YORK NOTES

LORD OF THE FLIES

WILLIAM GOLDING

NOTES BY S.W. FOSTER

D0963716

 Longman

Press

FOR GILL

ᴍᴛ(37)

The publishers wish to thank Arthur Bowden, former teaching colleague of
William Golding, for sharing his memories with the readers of these York Notes.

The right of S.W. Foster to be identified as Author of the Work
has been asserted by him in accordance with the
Copyright, Designs and Patents Act 1988

YORK PRESS
322 Old Brompton Road, London SW5 9JH

PEARSON EDUCATION LIMITED
Edinburgh Gate, Harlow,   OCT   2006
Essex CM20 2JE, United Kingdom
Associated companies, branches and representatives throughout the world

First published 1997
This new and fully revised edition first published 2002
Sixth impression 2006

10 9 8 7 6

ISBN-10: 0-582-50619-0
ISBN-13: 978-0-582-50619-0

Designed by Michelle Cannatella
Illustrations on pp. 14, 35, 50, 59, 60, 62, 63 and 65 by Anthea Toorchen
Illustrations on pp. 15, 18, 20, 29, 40, 42 and 47 by Hugh Abel
Map on p. 9 by Martin Ursell
Phototypeset by Gem Graphics, Trenance, Mawgan Porth, Cornwall
Colour reproduction and film output by Spectrum Colour
Produced by Pearson Education Asia Limited, Hong Kong

CONTENTS

PREFACE

York Notes are designed to give you a broader perspective on works of literature studied at GCSE and equivalent levels. With examination requirements changing in the twenty-first century, we have made a number of significant changes to this new series. We continue to help students to reach their own interpretations of the text but York Notes now have important extra-value new features.

You will discover that York Notes are genuinely interactive. The new **Checkpoint** features make sure that you can test your knowledge and broaden your understanding. You will also be directed to excellent websites, books and films where you can follow up ideas for yourself.

The **Resources** section has been updated and an entirely new section has been devoted to how to improve your grade. Careful reading and application of the principles laid out in the Resources section guarantee improved performance.

The **Detailed summaries** include an easy-to-follow skeleton structure of the story-line, while the section on **Language and style** has been extended to offer an in-depth discussion of the writer's techniques.

The Contents page shows the structure of this study guide. However, there is no need to read from the beginning to the end as you would with a novel, play or poem. Use the Notes in the way that suits you. Our aim is to help you with your understanding of the work, not to dictate how you should learn.

Our authors are practising English teachers and examiners who have used their experience to offer a whole range of **Examiner's secrets** – useful hints to encourage exam success.

The General Editor of this series is John Polley, Senior GCSE Examiner and former Head of English at Harrow Way Community School, Andover.

The author of these Notes is S.W. Foster B.Ed., M.A. (Ed.) who qualified in 1974 and has taught English in the state comprehensive system (11–16) since that time. He lives with his wife and three teenage children in Wiltshire.

The text used in these notes is the Faber and Faber edition, first published in paperback in 1958.

PART ONE

INTRODUCTION

HOW TO STUDY A NOVEL

A novelist starts with a story that examines a situation and the actions of particular characters. Remember that authors are not photographers, and that a novel never resembles real life exactly. Ultimately, a novel represents a view of the world that has been created in the author's imagination.

There are six features of a novel:

❶ THE STORY: this is the series of events, deliberately organised by the writer to test the characters

❷ THE CHARACTERS: the people who have to respond to the events of the story. Since they are human, they can be good or bad, clever or stupid, likeable or detestable, etc. They may change too!

❸ THE VIEWPOINT/VOICE: who is telling the story. The viewpoint may come from one of the characters, or from an omniscient (all-seeing) narrator, which allows the novelist to write about the perspectives of all the characters

❹ THE THEMES: these are the underlying messages, or meanings, of the novel

❺ THE SETTING: this concerns the time and place that the author has chosen for the story

❻ THE LANGUAGE AND STYLE: these are the words that the author has used to influence our understanding of the novel

To arrive at the fullest understanding of a novel, you need to read it several times. In this way, you can see how all the choices the author has made add up to a particular view of life, and develop your own ideas about it.

The purpose of these York Notes is to help you understand what the novel is about and to enable you to make your own interpretation. Do not expect the study of a novel to be neat and easy: novels are chosen for examination purposes, not written for them!

CHECK THE FILM

Lindsay Anderson's *If* (1968) is set in an English public school where dissatisfied pupils stage an armed uprising.

DID YOU KNOW?

Golding wrote much of this book while he was in class and teaching – in longhand and in school exercise books!

AUTHOR – LIFE AND WORKS	**CONTEXT**
1911 Born in Cornwall on 19 September, son of a schoolmaster at Marlborough College	**1914–18** First World War
1930 Brasenose College, Oxford studying Natural Sciences and English Literature	**1930** Stock Exchange crash
1934 Works as actor, producer and writer in small theatrical companies	
1939 Starts teaching at Bishop Wordsworth's School, Salisbury, Wiltshire. Serves in Royal Navy in command of a rocket ship, involved in the sinking of the Bismarck, the North Atlantic campaign and the Normandy invasion	**1939** Outbreak of Second World War
	1940 Battle of Britain
	1941–42 Battle for the North Atlantic
	1944 Allies invade Normandy on 4 June
1945 Returns to teach at Bishop Wordsworth's	**1945** Victory in Europe 8 May; Victory in Japan 15 August; Election of Labour Government
1954 Publication of *Lord of the Flies*	**1950–53** The Korean War
1955 Publishes *The Inheritors;* made Fellow of the Royal Society of Literature	**1951** Election of Churchill as PM
	1954 Start of Vietnam War
1956 Publishes *Pincher Martin*	**1956** The Suez Crisis
1959 Publishes *Free Fall*	
1961 Resigns from teaching to concentrate on writing	
	1962 Cuban Missile Crisis
1966 Awarded CBE	**1963** Assassination of J.F. Kennedy
1983 Nobel Prize for Literature	**1964** Election of Labour Government
1984 Made Companion of Literature	**1975** End of Vietnam as US pulls out
1988 Knighted	**1979** Election of Margaret Thatcher
1993 Dies on 19 June	**1990** The Gulf War

SETTING AND BACKGROUND

PERSONAL EXPERIENCES

Two important elements of Golding's life (1911–93) and experience are powerfully reflected in *Lord of the Flies* – his pessimism after the end of the Second World War and his insight, drawn from his life as a schoolmaster, into the way children behave and function.

On leaving university, Golding entered the teaching profession, where he remained until he enlisted in the Royal Navy at the start of the Second World War (1939–1945), during which he was promoted to commander and saw action which was to shock him into questioning the horror of war. These experiences inform his writing; he was appalled at what human beings can do to one another, not simply in terms of the Holocaust and other wartime atrocities, but in their being innately evil.

Golding returned to teaching in 1945 at Bishop Wordsworth School in Salisbury, Wiltshire. Although he wrote and pursued other interests, his writing alone was not enough to sustain him; he wrote chiefly for pleasure. The publication of *Lord of the Flies* (1954) did not release him from teaching, in financial terms, until 1962.

CHECK THE NET

Find a tribute to Golding at: www.geocities.com/ Athens/Forum/6249/ index.html/

SIN AND BRUTALITY

Historically, the post-war period was one of hope and optimism, but the events which Golding had witnessed did not allow him to see things so simplistically. The war alone was not what appalled him, but what he had learnt of the natural- and **original-sinfulness** of mankind did. It was the evil seen daily as commonplace and repeated by events it was possible to read in any newspaper which, he asserted, were the matter of *Lord of the Flies*. The war could be regarded as the catalyst which released an already present evil. People possessed this trait in a fundamental and permanent fashion – it could emerge at any time and under any conditions.

It was not just adults who had the capacity for brutality such as that seen in the German labour camps or in Japanese prisons. Golding isolates young children on the island in *Lord of the Flies* and allows us to see them acting with just as much barbarism as is revealed in the adult world. They are, in essence, innocent but nevertheless budding adults – and so potentially evil and sadistic. Children, it is said, can be cruel and in this novel we see stark examples of their cruelty.

THE BOYS

It is no accident that Jack and his choir come from a particularly rigid school background. Choir schools are by their nature elitist – probably every bit as much as the more severe public/private schools of that time. The organisation the boys were most familiar with would have been hierarchical, ordered and strict. Beatings, by boys and by masters, would have been commonplace. Without that strict regime and following such past conditioning, it is perhaps not surprising that Jack's deeper self is released in the way we witness.

Not all of the boys are from this culture, however, but the manner and tone of the boys is common in some marked respects. Their language (see **Language and style**), and to some extent their behaviour, is reminiscent of 1940s and 1950s comic books. Heroes like Roy of the Rovers and figures of fun like Frank Richards's Billy Bunter have clearly influenced the way in which Golding portrays the boys. They are initially, at least, similarly fun-loving, possessed of boyish good humour and a sense of natural decency. All of this is to change. Notice, too, how their language even under extreme provocation is relatively mild. It is also worth considering, in terms of culture and comparison, how a similar group of 1950s girls might have behaved in the same conditions and environment.

THE ISLAND

By its nature the island is isolated; there is no outside influence and nothing to distract the boys from their true natures. The island is self-sufficient and self-contained. It is a tropical Garden of Eden, complete with serpent.

Now take a break!

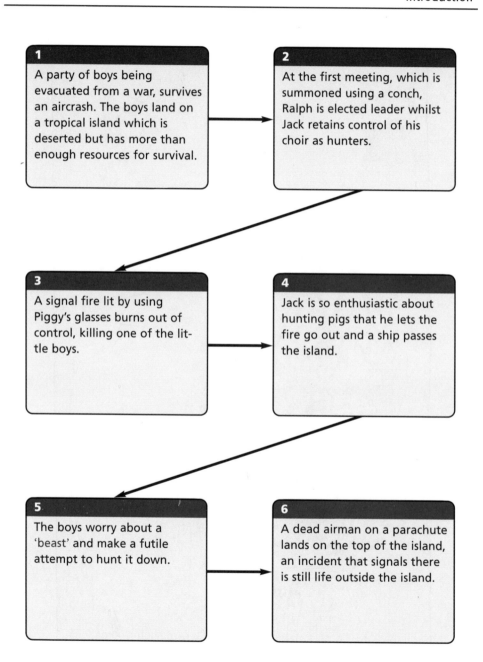

1

A party of boys being evacuated from a war, survives an aircrash. The boys land on a tropical island which is deserted but has more than enough resources for survival.

2

At the first meeting, which is summoned using a conch, Ralph is elected leader whilst Jack retains control of his choir as hunters.

3

A signal fire lit by using Piggy's glasses burns out of control, killing one of the little boys.

4

Jack is so enthusiastic about hunting pigs that he lets the fire go out and a ship passes the island.

5

The boys worry about a 'beast' and make a futile attempt to hunt it down.

6

A dead airman on a parachute lands on the top of the island, an incident that signals there is still life outside the island.

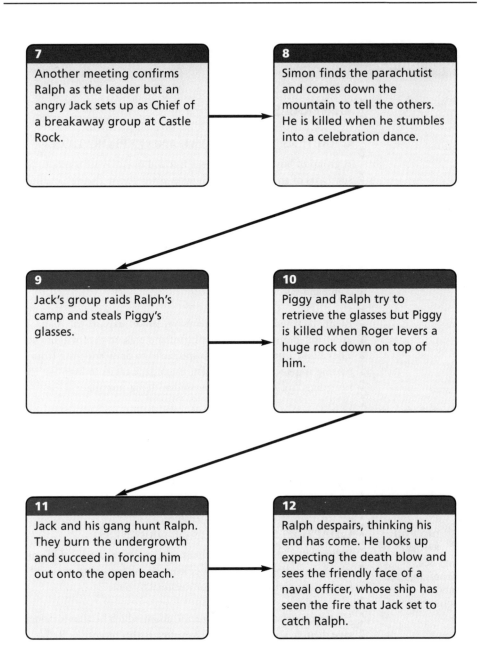

7

Another meeting confirms Ralph as the leader but an angry Jack sets up as Chief of a breakaway group at Castle Rock.

8

Simon finds the parachutist and comes down the mountain to tell the others. He is killed when he stumbles into a celebration dance.

9

Jack's group raids Ralph's camp and steals Piggy's glasses.

10

Piggy and Ralph try to retrieve the glasses but Piggy is killed when Roger levers a huge rock down on top of him.

11

Jack and his gang hunt Ralph. They burn the undergrowth and succeed in forcing him out onto the open beach.

12

Ralph despairs, thinking his end has come. He looks up expecting the death blow and sees the friendly face of a naval officer, whose ship has seen the fire that Jack set to catch Ralph.

PART TWO

SUMMARIES

GENERAL SUMMARY

CHAPTERS 1–4 – ARRIVAL AND EXPLORATION

A group of boys – aged between five and twelve – are the sole survivors of an air crash which takes place during their evacuation from England.

Having landed on a fictitious tropical island, two of the boys, Ralph and Piggy, use a conch to announce their presence. Other boys come in answer to the call, including a group of choir boys headed by Jack. Ralph is chosen as leader in preference to Jack, who is allowed to command his choir as hunters.

Ralph, Jack and one of the choirboys, Simon, explore the island. It is uninhabited but it has plenty of fruit and pigs, so they will not starve. They build a fire using Piggy's spectacles to draw attention from passing ships which could rescue them. Jack offers to keep the rescue fire going, but he becomes obsessed with pig-hunting.

While Jack is out hunting, Ralph thinks he can see smoke from a ship's funnel. He rushes to the signal fire, only to find that it has gone out. Meanwhile, Jack returns from his first successful hunt to be rebuked for letting the fire go out. In his guilt, he punches Piggy, breaking one lens of his glasses. The boys cook the pig and, in celebration of their hunt, they retell and act out the event.

DID YOU KNOW?

Twenty-one publishers rejected Golding's manuscript of this book.

CHAPTERS 5–8 – BEASTS OF DARKNESS

Ralph calls a meeting and outlines some practical details of life on the island, including the necessity of keeping the fire going, the need for fresh water and shelters and for personal hygiene.

He then touches on another matter, about which he allows them to give their views – 'the beast'. Dismayed by his reception, Ralph considers stepping down as chief and wishes for a sign of some sort from the outside world.

A sign arrives in the form of a dead airman, who descends in a parachute and is assumed to be the beast. In the hunt for the beast, the boys discover an outcrop of rock which would make a good fort.

Ralph, Jack and Roger go to the mountain – where the beast was last seen. Like Sam and Eric, they see something vaguely in the darkness which frightens them and they run away.

At a subsequent meeting, Jack is thwarted in his efforts to become chief and storms off to set up on his own. He is joined by other boys who kill a pig and leave its severed head as a gift for the beast.

Simon is in the forest during the kill and talks with the head of the pig as if it understands him. Later he falls unconscious.

CHAPTERS 9–12 – DEATH AND DISCOVERY

Simon wakes up; he is certain that the truth about the beast is to be found on the mountain. He finds the body of the pilot. Meanwhile, Jack's group has moved to another camp. Piggy and Ralph visit them to have some meat. The celebration dance becomes violent just as Simon arrives with news of the airman and he is killed.

Jack's group raids Ralph's party and steals Piggy's glasses. Piggy is killed in an ensuing incident.

Ralph hides in the jungle and awakens to the sound of the hunters, who roll two more rocks into the bushes in order to flush him out. Breaking out of the undergrowth, he makes for the beach but, exhausted, he stumbles and falls.

Instead of the expected death blows, Ralph looks up to the puzzled gaze of a Royal Navy officer who has seen the smoke and come to rescue the boys.

 CHECK THE NET
An interesting website on the novel can be found at:
www.gerenser. com/lotf

Now take a break!

DETAILED SUMMARIES

CHAPTER 1 – The Sound of the Shell

1 A group of boys is marooned on an island.

2 Piggy and Ralph are first on the scene and use a conch which summons other survivors.

3 The most impressive entrance is made by a group of choirboys under Jack Merrdiew, the head choirboy.

4 One of the choirboys, Simon, faints.

5 A meeting now elects Ralph as chief.

6 Piggy's nickname is revealed to the boys' general amusement.

7 Ralph, Jack and Simon decide to explore the island.

CHECKPOINT 1

What is the correct pronunciation of conch?

During evacuation following a period of hostility in England, a group of boys find themselves marooned on an island. Two of the boys, Ralph and Piggy, are struggling through the island's undergrowth, anxious after their sudden arrival to find adult help and fellow passengers. They appear dazed and confused about what eventually happened to the plane. As yet, they have found no one except each other.

Ralph is clearly more relaxed about the situation than Piggy, taking the opportunity to go for a swim in the tropical heat. Piggy attempts to make Ralph's acquaintance, confiding to him that Piggy is a nickname (that he would prefer was kept a secret), along with other information about his background. In a lagoon Ralph spots a shell which Piggy immediately identifies as a conch. He tutors Ralph in how to blow it in order to make a sound to call the other survivors.

As the sound of the conch booms across the island, boys begin to emerge slowly. They include a line of choirboys in strange attire.

On arrival at the meeting place, one of the boys – Simon – collapses from the heat. The head chorister – Jack Merridew – ignoring his fainted companion, enquires if there are any adult survivors. When he discovers that there are not, he suggests that they fend for themselves. Piggy agrees and proposes that they make a list of names – he has already made a start – but Jack ridicules his list as being 'Kid's names … Why should I be Jack? I'm Merridew' (p. 17). Clearly not keen to be on first name terms, he criticises 'Fatty' for being too talkative and is corrected by Ralph who says the fat boy's name is Piggy.

DID YOU KNOW?

Golding was an accomplished musician with a fine tenor voice.

When the laughter has faded, Jack says they ought to think about being rescued. Ralph feels they need a chief – a role which Jack, arrogantly, assumes for himself despite the fact that, as Piggy points out, Ralph called the meeting using the conch.

After a vote, Ralph is elected leader or 'chief' (p. 18) and, diplomatically, concedes that Jack is still responsible for the choir who might double as an army or hunters. Ralph selects Jack and Simon to accompany him, in order to discover whether they are indeed on an island or just a promontory of land.

CHECKPOINT 2

How does Ralph soften the blow for Jack when he is not elected chief?

Before the boys leave, Piggy remonstrates with Ralph about telling the group his name. Ralph apologises and gives Piggy the task of taking the boys' names.

Ralph, Jack and Simon tackle the job of exploration with boyish enthusiasm, eventually discovering that they really are on a picturesque tropical island, complete with lagoon, reefs, mountain and jungle. On their return they find a piglet caught in the creepers. Jack draws his knife to kill it, but cannot do so.

> **The island**
>
> The island setting is described in vivid, physical terms. It is clearly a tropical paradise. Notice the words the author uses to portray its richness and variety – 'reef', 'cirque', 'scar', 'lagoon', 'defile'. Notice as you read the book that the island is one of many contrasts – high and low, rocky and forested, friendly and unfriendly. It is also 'roughly boat-shaped' (p. 26) – tapering towards one end. Continuing the idea of first principles, an author does not choose characters or setting purely by chance – they all have a deliberate function.

The initial impact of the first chapter in any novel is important – it should be full of possibilities and encourage you to anticipate and predict what might happen later. Many Shakespeare plays contain within the first act all the information and ingredients for later action. The same is sometimes true of fiction. Although your predictions may not be right, you may be able to trace later events back to a point which might explain the reasons behind an action or type of behaviour.

The descriptions of the principal characters are intended to conjure up an impression in your mind. Golding creates a clear, early contrast between Ralph and Piggy. The character of Jack is also strongly drawn. Simon features in relatively small but nevertheless significant ways. These four characters are to be the key to the novel.

The names given to the boys are of some significance, albeit slight. Most of the boys have names which were common and popular before and just after the Second World War. Piggy is so named because of his appearance – we never know his true name. Only two names are of biblical origin or saints' names. These are Simon (the apostle who carried Christ's cross and was later martyred) and John (a common form of which is Jack).

CHAPTER 2 – Fire on the Mountain

① The explorers return and call a meeting.

② The young ones worry about a beast.

③ They agree to start a fire to attract attention.

④ The fire burns out of control.

⑤ The boy with the birthmark disappears.

The three explorers return and Ralph blows the conch to call the other boys to the meeting platform. Uncertainly at first, then with growing confidence, he explains that they are on an uninhabited island. They have found no evidence of any human presence – however slight.

Jack stresses the logical need, as he sees it, for hunters, particularly as they have found pigs which could provide them with meat. Ralph continues to explain more pressing points, firstly that whoever holds the conch is empowered to speak, so that discussions remain orderly. Second, as there are no adults the boys must fend for themselves. Ralph also reassures the boys that they will be rescued but, as no one knows exactly where they are, this could take a while. The island is one that can provide for their needs so they can survive comparatively easily and also have some fun in the meantime.

During the meeting a six-year-old boy with a birthmark asks diffidently, through Piggy, what they intend doing about 'a beastie' or 'snake thing' he has seen (p. 34). Ralph says there would not be any such thing on an island of this size. The other boys dismiss the little boy's claims as a dream or his imagination brought on by seeing the creepers. Jack, claiming the conch, says he and his

> **CHECKPOINT 3**
>
> Is the island too small for both Jack and Ralph?

group will ensure that there is not a snake when they go hunting. Although the fears about the beastie/snake thing are rejected wholesale by the boys, nevertheless a seed of apprehension is planted. Observe how this reservation grows in the later chapters.

Ralph shows his simple faith that they will be rescued – but thinks they could help the process by lighting a fire to produce smoke to attract a passing ship. This idea appeals to the boys, fulfilling both their wish for rescue and their natural lust for fun and adventure. They rush off up the mountain to gather wood. Piggy follows reluctantly, disgusted by their lack of order and foresight. The boys work energetically to gather a pile of wood, but see no way of lighting it. Jack happens on the idea of using Piggy's glasses to magnify the rays of the sun. The wood is dry and rotten, so a flame is quickly kindled.

DID YOU KNOW?

Golding was embarrassed about his poems published in 1934. When he found a book of his poems in a second-hand bookshop, he bought it for 6d and burned it at home.

The boys continue to feed the fire, producing not signal smoke but flame. They decide to put on green branches to make smoke and determine to keep the fire going – Jack offering his choir/hunters to work in rotation at the task.

Unfortunately, the fire rages out of hand, burning through a large swathe of forest. Piggy becomes firstly frightened at the power that has been unleashed in the fire, then angry at the boys' stupidity and lack of foresight. He also expresses concern for the welfare of the smaller boys – 'the littluns' – and counters Ralph's rebuke at his lack of ability to collect their names by saying that they just keep running off.

Pointing out their lack of care for the island's population of boys, Piggy cites the example of the little boy with the birthmark who is nowhere to be found. The boys feel guilt and shame at his possible fate.

The fire and Piggy

The fire has two purposes – it is a practical aid to the boys' rescue and a source of fun. Under normal circumstances boys between six and twelve years of age would not be entrusted with fire, even with adult supervision, and certainly not on this scale. Notice how the atmosphere changes when the fire becomes not fun but fatal.

Piggy supports Ralph in this chapter. Ralph has explained their predicament and suggests the idea of the fire, but even he does not follow the idea through. It is Piggy who explains the need for smoke not flame. There is an **irony** in the fact that although his sight is poor ('Jus' blurs, that's all. Hardly see my hand' [p. 40]) his foresight (perception and understanding of the consequences of actions) is excellent. Further, while the boys see the potential for enjoyment in the fire, Piggy sees its potential dangers. His manner and tone in this chapter are almost parental ('My! You've made a big heap, haven't you?' [p. 40]). He also urges the need for practical considerations, like shelters, after the cold of the previous night.

CHECKPOINT 4

What happens to the boy with the birthmark?

CHAPTER 3 – Huts on the Beach

1 Jack goes pig-hunting – unsuccessfully.
2 The boys begin to erect shelters.
3 Simon goes off on his own.

The chapter begins with Jack tracking pigs through the undergrowth. He uses all of his senses but, even with this heightened awareness, when he gets close enough his attempt at a kill is unsuccessful. He gives up after his abortive efforts and returns to the lagoon. Why is Jack intent on hunting and killing the pigs? Is it because of a sense of failure that he did not kill one immediately when he came across it during the exploration?

> **CHECKPOINT 5**
>
> Why is Jack so keen for meat on an island rich in fruit and shellfish?

Ralph is concerned with practical matters: mainly the fire and constructing the shelters. His actions follow the dictates of the assembly, while virtually everyone else is doing what they want. This indicates something about his sense of responsibility and concern for the overall welfare of the boys on the island. Unfortunately, his shelter-building has been no more successful than Jack's hunting.

The other boys, including Jack's hunters, have disappeared to swim, eat or play and have given very little assistance. Ralph is rather scathing about Jack's failure to get meat and is bitter about the lack of help with the shelters. He resents the time he has put in trying to build them in order that the boys have protection if it rains – and from the beast.

Ralph and Jack dismiss the idea of the 'beastie' as ridiculous. Jack, however, admits to feeling some fear when he is hunting, saying that he feels as if he is being hunted himself. Ralph says that the best way to avoid fear of any sort is to be rescued, and emphasises the importance of the fire. Jack, on the other hand, continues to express his enthusiasm for hunting the pigs and obtaining meat. He reasons that the pigs must shelter from the heat of the day on the flatter part of the island. Jack's unceasing fascination with the pigs irritates Ralph. He feels he is doing something out of necessity while Jack is doing something for fun. Ralph complains that he only has Simon's help.

During their discussion Simon – who, it seems, is always around – has wandered off, supposedly to go for a swim. Ralph and Jack go to the bathing pool. Simon has walked along the beach and up the scar. Urged by some of the younger boys to pick fruit from the higher branches, he helps them. Leaving the boys to eat, Simon goes off into the jungle on his own.

CHECKPOINT 6

What evidence is there that Jack is fully focused on hunting?

Simon emerges as a character

Again Simon plays a part in this chapter and we learn further information about him. He is repeatedly referred to as being strange in one way or another, but exactly what form this takes is never very certain. He is helpful in building the shelters and finding food for the littluns but also content to sit alone in the forest. The younger boys follow him about, which seems to show that he is popular in spite of Ralph's view of him as an oddity.

At this stage, the fire is still seen as being of importance. Fire is an essential part of any possible rescue. As the story progresses, certain characters consider it vital while for others it becomes gradually less important. Some of the boys are interested only in things of immediate significance and some merely subsist, that is live from day to day and have no view of future events or prospects.

Piggy is, perhaps surprisingly, not in evidence in this chapter. He is seen in the next chapter as someone who, in Ralph's eyes, is not a worker and so may have avoided any involvement in the shelter-building.

CHAPTER 4 – Painted Faces and Long Hair

❶ The littluns play on the beach.

❷ Jack goes off hunting.

❸ Ralph sees the smoke of a ship on the horizon.

❹ He discovers the fire has gone out.

❺ The hunters return with a dead pig.

❻ Ralph is angry and calls a meeting.

The boys have become almost used to the rhythm of the tropical day – and the mirages produced by the heat – but the pattern of life they are most familiar with prevents them from accepting this new rhythm completely. The boys are described as falling into three broad categories: 'the biguns' (Ralph, Jack, Piggy and Simon), graduating through a vague middle region (which includes Robert and Maurice) to 'the littluns' (p. 61). This last group – of around six years of age – are denoted as being tanned, dirty, afflicted with stomach problems and prone to nightmares. They spend their time eating, sleeping or playing absorbedly.

In the early part of this chapter, patterns of behaviour have become settled into a daily routine: the way the boys have become pigeon-holed into groups and initial impressions of the characters are now crystallised. On the other hand, elements of that same behaviour are magnified and enlarged as the chapter progresses.

CHECKPOINT 7

Who mimics Roger's cruelty?

Three littluns – Henry, Percival and Johnny – are portrayed during one of their games. Roger and Maurice pass them, destroying their sandcastle and kicking sand in Percival's eye. The older boys, it seems, feel only a tinge of guilt. Percival recovers, only to have his younger companions repeat the cruelty.

Roger watches all this and continues his observation as Henry wanders away and becomes fascinated by some minute, transparent sea creatures brought in by the surf. Roger teases him by throwing stones to land close while he, Roger, is concealed behind a tree.

Jack arrives, having found some clay to use as facial camouflage, and explains that he believes the pigs see him rather than smell his scent. He smears his face and goes off to hunt.

At the bathing pool Ralph considers Piggy in a negative light and recognises him to be an outsider and an irritation. Suddenly, Ralph believes he can see the smoke from a ship's funnel. He is badly scratched as he dashes through the undergrowth in an effort to reach the signal fire – only to discover that it has gone out. Ralph shouts to the disappearing ship in an expression of his total despair.

The hunters return, chanting in triumph having killed a pig. Ralph, at odds with the torrent of enthusiasm, states that the signal fire was out when there was a ship passing. Eventually, Jack realises the futility of hunting against the possibility of rescue. Unable to face the barrage of supporting comments from Piggy, he punches him, breaking one lens of his glasses.

> **CHECKPOINT 8**
>
> What difference is there in the reactions of Ralph and Jack to missing the ship?

Jack apologises grudgingly for letting the fire go out. It is then relit, using the remaining lens in Piggy's spectacles. The boys cook the pig and Ralph is forced out of his silence to accept some meat. Piggy asks for some but Jack points out that he is not entitled to any because he did not hunt. Simon, guilty at not having hunted either, gives his meat to Piggy. Jack is infuriated at this apparent ingratitude shown towards his hard work and generosity. He glories in retelling the story of the hunt and some of the boys re-enact the kill, in primitive style. Ralph, unable to come to terms with their failure to contact the ship, decides to call a meeting.

A gradual de-civilising process is emerging. Evidence of this can be seen in the lack of cleanliness over eating and personal hygiene. The same deterioration is noticeable in the way that Roger's unkindness is copied by Maurice and then repeated by the littluns. Although Maurice feels some shame at his actions, he quickly forgets about what he has done because there are no adults present to punish him. Finally, the hunters' response to their successful kill is both primitive and pagan, complete with tribal dance, **tri-syllabic chanting** and a simplistic replay of the whole event.

The growing gap between Ralph and Jack

Jack is determined and single-minded in his pursuit of the pigs yet proud and pugnacious in the incident involving Piggy. He apologises for letting the fire go out but not, significantly, for breaking the glasses. He lashes out at Piggy partly because he is embarrassed at the truth of his omission, but also because he feels cornered. The apology is a painful – and unusual – experience for him.

Ralph exhibits real despair at the passing of the ship, possibly because he is beginning to feel the pressure of his overall responsibility for the boys. He has also been involved in work, building the shelters, and the idea that the island is fun is wearing thin. He is also beginning to re-assess the usefulness of his fellow-castaways. In the next chapter, however, Ralph's low opinion of Piggy ('Piggy was a bore' [p. 68]) alters.

Now take a break!

WHO SAYS ...?

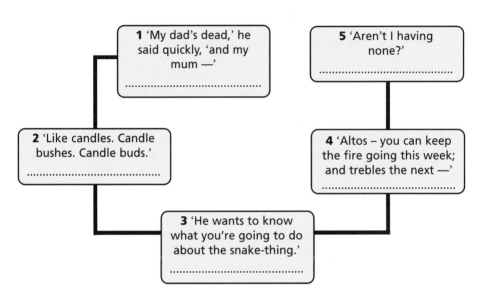

1 'My dad's dead,' he said quickly, 'and my mum —'

....

5 'Aren't I having none?'

....

2 'Like candles. Candle bushes. Candle buds.'

....

4 'Altos – you can keep the fire going this week; and trebles the next —'

....

3 'He wants to know what you're going to do about the snake-thing.'

....

ABOUT WHOM?

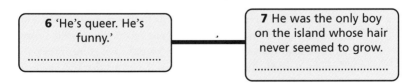

6 'He's queer. He's funny.'

....

7 He was the only boy on the island whose hair never seemed to grow.

....

Check your answers on p. 84.

CHAPTER 5 – Beast from Water

1 **At the meeting Ralph lays down the ground rules.**

2 **Jack asserts that the beast is a product of the imagination.**

3 **The opinions of Piggy and Simon are ignored.**

4 **Jack storms off from the meeting.**

After missing the ship and the signal fire going out because of Jack and the boys' preoccupation with hunting, life for Ralph takes on a new seriousness. He walks on the beach considering the boys' initial enthusiasm for the island, how their original ideas for keeping order had broken down, and the poor prospects of imminent rescue. Having decided to call an assembly, he is anxious that it does not degenerate into a pointless fiasco, as it has previously. He thinks beforehand, 'This meeting must not be fun, but business' (p. 81).

As the boys gather there is an air of solemnity even over those who did not witness Ralph's anger about the fire going out. The atmosphere is additionally sombre because it is much later in the day than the meetings are usually held. Before starting to speak, Ralph considers the weight of his responsibilities as chief. He recognises the ability to think rationally and systematically as an important requirement for a leader. He also realises that Piggy has the capacity for clear thinking and begins to regard his fat companion with new-found respect.

CHECKPOINT 9

What particularly worries Ralph about the boys' adjustment to life on the island?

Ralph opens the meeting by setting out ground rules about how it is to be conducted, so that nothing spoils the impact of the few simple points he wishes to make. In a plain, ordered fashion he raises five issues which he feels are central to their survival and well-being. The first four are practical matters which provoke little discussion or argument. He explains: the need for fresh water; the need for shelters to be built; the necessity of using one agreed place as a lavatory; and, most important of all, the need to keep the fire going if they are ever to be rescued. As their elected chief, he insists that these rules are adhered to.

The fifth and final item on Ralph's agenda is 'the fear' or 'the beastie' (p. 88). It is the only matter on which he will allow discussion and, understandably, the only matter about which many of the boys are unable to express their feelings. Jack, now regarded as a proven hunter, discounts the notion of the beast being a real, tangible creature. Having been all over the island and having found nothing larger than pigs, he regards the idea as nonsense. The beast is therefore, he argues, intangible – a product of the littluns' imagination – and he berates them for their cowardice. Piggy agrees with Jack, in part. He too rejects the idea of the beast being a real thing – using his knowledge of science and natural logic. He also dismisses the notion of the beast being a creature of the imagination, but does so with sympathy and understanding. The only fear worth considering is the fear of people.

At this point one of the littluns comes forward and admits to having a nightmare and to seeing something moving about in the forest. It turns out that it could have been Simon, who is then rebuked for frightening the littluns. Another little boy – Percival Wemys Madison – is coaxed by Piggy into telling his story. Unfortunately he ultimately dissolves in tears which produce near-hysteria in the other younger boys. It is only Maurice's clowning and his return to the subject of the beast that enables order to be restored. His mention of giant squid, however, produces further distress and Ralph blows the conch for silence. Simon feels the need to speak and takes the conch but has neither the language, nor the opportunity, to express his notions of evil.

> **CHECKPOINT 10**
>
> Why might Piggy be fearful of people?

The signficance of the beast

Although the chapter is called 'Beast from Water', in 'deciding on the fear' (p. 88) a number of explanations are put forward. These range from real wild creatures, like the giant squid, to human beings as a source of fear. Unreal phenomena are also considered – fear created by the imagination, fear of evil and fear of the supernatural in the form of ghosts. Notice how each suggestion is received by the different boys.

Piggy's attempt to discount the existence of ghosts is interrupted by Jack and then put to the vote by Ralph. In the gloom it is difficult to assess the outcome, but Piggy still insists that ghosts do not exist. Jack's contempt for Piggy and his lack of respect for the authority of the conch and Ralph as leader lead him to disregard the rules.

Jack leaves and the assembly breaks up in disarray. Ralph, Piggy and Simon remain to consider their problems. Ralph contemplates giving up as chief. Piggy fears for his own position if Ralph were to relinquish his title. They all long for adult support and wish they could be sent 'a sign or something' (p. 102) from the outside world. Their thoughts are disturbed by Percival Wemys Madison crying in the darkness.

This chapter marks the beginnings of a break in the relationship between Ralph and Jack and the division of the boys on the island into two factions.

CHAPTER 6 – Beast from Air

❶ A dead parachutist lands on the island.

❷ Sam and Eric believe it is the beast.

❸ At a meeting Jack announces it should be hunted down.

❹ The bigger boys, without Piggy, set off to find the beast.

❺ They discover a good place for a fort at the end of the island.

Ralph and Simon carry Percival to one of the shelters and eventually they all fall asleep. Ten miles above them a battle is being fought and a 'sign … from the world of grown-ups' (p. 103) comes down in the form of a parachutist.

CHECKPOINT 11

What is the significance of the parachutist?

He lands on the mountain where the breeze and the parachute's suspension lines control his body like the strings of a puppet. Sam and Eric have been on duty at the fire but have almost allowed it to go out. In the early morning darkness, while trying to rekindle the fire, Eric hears the sound of the parachute canopy. Neither boy can see very clearly and, believing they have encountered 'the beast', they run away in terror.

They report the sighting to Ralph who, conscious of the near panic of the previous evening, tells them to call an assembly as calmly and quietly as possible. However, Sam and Eric, speaking as one, give a description which is both terrifying – because it is reinforced by duplication – and reassuring – because now it is recognised as real.

Their mention of the beast's teeth and claws, its eyes and the way it 'kind of sat up' (p. 109) leave the other boys in no doubt that the beast is a tangible thing which can, therefore, be hunted.

Jack is ecstatic at the prospect of a hunt and Piggy, for all his dismissal of the fear of ghosts the previous evening, admits to being frightened. He suggests that they stay where they are in the hope that the beast will not come near them. Ralph points out that it would not, therefore, be possible to fetch food and details Piggy to look after the littluns. Piggy takes the conch in order to explain that he is frightened and of little use with his broken glasses. Jack interrupts to ridicule both Piggy's fear and the importance of the conch.

He says that the ritual of holding it to speak to the assembly is pointless and unproductive. The atmosphere is tense as Ralph reaffirms the value of the conch and his own leadership by telling Jack to sit down. Ralph then takes control of the situation by saying

CHECKPOINT 12

What does the conch symbolise?

that the beast leaves no tracks and cannot be hunted in the normal way. He reminds the boys of the importance of rescue as their top priority. They will therefore search for the beast in the tail end of the island – the only part that Jack has not visited – then return to the mountain to re-light the fire.

Leaving Piggy and the littluns behind, Ralph and the bigger boys go in search of the beast with Jack in the lead. As they walk along, Simon reflects on his inability to speak to the group about his ideas about the beast. He then has a vision of the beast as 'a human at once heroic and sick' (p. 112).

DID YOU KNOW?

Golding was an avid reader of books on psychology.

Arriving at the tail end of the island, even Jack is apprehensive. Ralph takes the initiative, as leader, to go forward alone, comforted by Simon's reassurance that there is no beast. He discovers nothing but an outcrop of rock which Jack, following shortly after him, says would make an ideal fort. Ralph insists that they return and light the fire on the mountain. Many of the boys want to stay at the fort and play, or roll rocks off the outcrop into the sea, but Ralph forcefully reminds them of the importance of the signal fire. Unwillingly they leave the outcrop, led by Jack.

Ralph's courage

Ralph shows a degree of common sense and an almost obsessive determination in this chapter. He attempts, despite the undercurrent of resentment from Jack, to push through some of the points he made during the previous night's assembly. He shows courage in ultimately leading the exploration of the far end of the island, and moral courage in facing up to Jack over the supremacy of the conch.

Despite Jack's bravado and Piggy's theorising, neither of them shows the courage of his convictions. Jack is keen to hunt the beast but finally cannot do so. Piggy is intellectually convinced that ghosts do not exist but declares his fear of the beast and stays to look after the littluns.

Simon emerges once again as a complex and important minor character. Despite the fact that he says and does comparatively little, his speech and actions are highly significant. Take careful note of what happens whenever his name is mentioned.

The discovery of the outcrop of rock at the end of the island is relevant to later action in the novel. While Jack enthuses about its possibilities as a fort, Ralph senses something evil in the enormity of the ocean which surges around the island at that point. This place is later known as Castle Rock.

CHAPTER 7 – Shadows and Tall Trees

❶ Ralph is dismayed by the state of the boys.

❷ Jack discovers the tracks of a wild boar.

❸ The boys devise a ritual dance to celebrate the hunt.

❹ Ralph, Jack and Roger climb to the top of the island and discover the dead parachutist.

❺ Terrified by their discovery, they flee down the mountain.

DID YOU KNOW?

Golding's nickname as a teacher was 'Scruff'.

The boys follow Jack along the pig run, and the sound of the sea in the afternoon sun allows Ralph to forget the beast. He asks Jack to stop when they come to some fruit trees so that the boys can eat. As they take a break, Ralph considers the filthy state of his shirt and contemplates washing it. He also feels he needs to have a bath and clean his teeth. He is alarmed at the fact that he has resorted to the childish habit of biting his nails and wonders aloud whether he will soon start sucking his thumb. Once again – see pp. 85–6 – Ralph considers the subject of cleanliness and reviews the state of the other boys. They too are dirty, their hair tangled, their clothing worn and stiff with sweat. Ralph is a little shocked that he now regards these conditions as normal.

Turning from the boys, Ralph is awed by the immensity and power of the ocean – which he sees as a barrier between the island and the civilised world. Simon, with great insight, correctly interprets Ralph's silent reverie as a longing to return home and reassures him that he will get there, eventually.

CHECKPOINT 13

What is the value of Simon's imagination?

Roger discovers some pig droppings and Jack suggests that it would be convenient to hunt the pig at the same time as they were hunting 'the other thing' (p. 122) – the beast. Ralph agrees, conceding, in his own mind, that they will eventually get back to the mountain.

As Jack tracks the pig, Ralph has time to cast his mind back to the comforts of his typical English, middle-class home. He is jolted out of his reflections by the sound of a pig. He throws his spear, hitting the boar on the nose and so diverting it. They follow the boar and Ralph, caught up in the excitement of the hunt, prides himself on his achievement, only to be rebuked by Jack – who has sustained a minor injury – for not throwing more effectively.

In retelling his part in the hunt, Ralph inadvertently incites the boys into performing a playful re-enactment of it – complete with chant. Although Robert, who represents the pig, is only slightly hurt, Ralph experiences something of the frenzy and blood lust of the hunters (see **Crowd mentality** in **Themes**). Jack suggests getting one of the boys to dress up as a pig and jokes about using the littluns for the purpose.

Ralph raises the subject of going to the mountain and starting the fire, but is reminded that they do not have Piggy's glasses. He proposes that they follow the coastline to the mountain and climb up it through the burnt area. This turns out to be difficult; they encounter impenetrable forest which forces them down to a dangerous course at the cliff edge. Ralph pauses to consider his wider responsibilities to Piggy and the littluns. Simon volunteers to go back through the forest to them.

CHECKPOINT 14

What is the source of the rising tension between Jack and Ralph?

Ralph questions Jack about his explorations to find out where they are in relation to the pig run. Jack responds that the pig run is close by, below the mountain. They decide to push through the forest to get to it.

Jack and Ralph vie with each other, each trying to prove his own courage and right to the leadership. Jack, already resentful of Ralph, must, it seems, achieve the summit of the mountain in order to save face after his apparent cowardice at Castle Rock. Jack has not been quite so thorough in his exploration of the island as he claims.

Ralph is better able to think now; at one point thinking aloud quite unashamedly. The ability to think is openly attributed to Piggy. Ralph recognises that Jack hates him – but does not understand why – with the 'new understanding that Piggy had given him' (p. 129).

When put to the vote, all but Ralph, Jack and Roger decide to return to Piggy at the platform. The three boys push on through the burnt patch of forest and Jack, perhaps shamed by the reminder of his earlier behaviour, goes on to the mountain top while Ralph and Roger wait in silence. Jack eventually returns, clearly shocked – despite his bravado – by having seen something 'bulge' and heard it 'plop' (p. 133). Ralph leads the boys to the mountain top to see the almost indistinguishable hump which Jack has described. Suddenly, the clouds shift from in front of the moon, the wind roars – so that the parachute moves the body – and the 'creature lifted its head' revealing 'something like a great ape' (p. 135). The boys leave the mountain in haste.

Tribal dance

The enactment of the hunt is reminiscent of tribal dances, which are a ritualistic representation of a successful hunt that the tribe hopes for in the future. This, coupled with Jack's mask and the rallying chant of earlier chapters, highlights the move away from conventional behaviour.

Natural images and descriptions abound in this chapter. Ralph's continuing thoughts about the vastness of the sea – see Ch. 6 – are repeated at greater length. The description of the forest is vivid; the undergrowth on one side is impassable, the sea and cliffs on the other are threatening. The final revelation of the beast is effected by natural forces.

The dramatic visual image at the end of the chapter, with the moon and the wind together conspiring to reveal the beast, has a suitably dynamic impact on the three boys.

 DID YOU KNOW?
Golding used to read the chapters of *Lord of the Flies* as he finished them to his Year 11 English class – and get them to do the proofreading for him!

CHAPTER 8 – Gift for the Darkness

1 The three boys report their encounter with the beast.

2 The meeting rejects Jack as the new chief.

3 The fire is re-lit.

4 Jack goes off with his hunters to kill pigs.

5 They sever the pig's head and put it on a stick on the beach.

6 Simon returns and meditates on the nature of the head.

7 The hunters feast on their own.

The boys return and tell about the sighting of the beast. Piggy questions Ralph closely about it and, from Ralph's responses, concludes that they would be powerless against such a creature. Jack counters by saying that it might be tackled by his hunters. Ralph is contemptuous, describing them as 'Boys armed with sticks' (p. 137). Jack is hurt by Ralph's dismissal of his hunters and blows the conch to call a meeting – which Ralph says he had intended to do anyway.

It is now common knowledge that the three boys have seen the beast. Jack maintains that it is 'a hunter' (p. 138) – although on what evidence is unclear. Ralph, he says, has insulted his hunters; Ralph is not a proper chief and has shown himself to be cowardly. After a brief volley of argument Jack gets to the main thrust of his speech and holds a vote of no confidence in Ralph's leadership. No one votes to remove Ralph as leader so, for the second time, Jack is unsuccessful. (On this occasion, not even the choir vote for him.) In his anger and frustration at this, Jack walks off in tearful fury to set up on his own.

Ralph is bewildered by Jack's reaction and feels that he will come back in the evening. Piggy, however, is pleased and relieved at Jack's departure. He says that there will be no need for Jack and his hunters now, and that the boys must stay near the platform to avoid the beast – about which he is still sceptical. Simon shyly and hesitantly suggests that they should climb the mountain. Typically, the boys ignore him.

CHECK THE NET

A range of past and present front covers for the novel can be viewed at: **lordoftheflies. org/book.html**. Which do you think is the most effective and why?

Piggy brings up the matter of the fire and proffers the suggestion that they light it by the bathing pool instead of on the mountain.

The boys set to build the fire with a sense of purpose, using rather damp wood, and Piggy takes the initiative for once to light it. With the fire lit, Piggy and Ralph consider reorganising things and making a list of names, only to find that many of the boys have drifted away. It is suspected that these, like Jack, were the troublemakers who did not want to 'play' (p. 144).

Ralph feels that they will be better off on their own. Piggy, Sam and Eric collect some fruit, which is eaten in an atmosphere of celebration. They discover that Simon too has disappeared, they suspect to climb the mountain. He has in fact gone off to sit in solitude.

Meanwhile, Jack has gathered a group of boys that he is going to lead as chief. He tells them that they will forget about the beast, kill a pig and have a feast at Castle Rock. The boys move off to the forest to hunt. They find a sow with her piglets and kill her. The atmosphere, both tense and violent, is broken only by Maurice's coarse humour and another – this time amusing – re-enactment of the hunt.

> **CHECKPOINT 15**
>
> What are Piggy's feelings when Jack departs?

DID YOU KNOW?

Golding lived for a while at Broadchalke near Salisbury. His neighbour and close friend was James Lovelock, the inventor of the microwave oven.

The split between Jack and Ralph and the establishment of the conch group and the hunters as separate entities could be anticipated. It is a natural development of the differences between the two main characters. The ethos of the conch group is in marked contrast to that of the hunters, who are primarily interested in having fun. The hunters behave in a primitive fashion – wear paint, use spears, are virtually naked and live for the moment. Significantly, they have no conch or other object to regulate who speaks and when. On the contrary, Jack's announcement is reinforced by two hunters in a stylised and rehearsed afterword – 'The Chief has spoken' (p. 155) – which prevents further argument.

Jack guts the pig and, in his capacity as 'Chief', instructs the boys to take the meat to the platform. He also divulges his plan to raid the other group to get some fire. They put the pig's head on a stick as a gift for the beast and leave the forest to return to the beach.

The Lord of the Flies

There are references in ancient history to a 'god of the flies' being worshipped by pagan civilisations. Although Jack has said that they are going to forget about the beast, the pig's head is still left as a gift to placate it. There is a grudging acceptance of, and respect for, this unnamed being which has been raised to the status of deity. The pig's head is left as a sacrifice in gratitude for a successful hunt. There is a parallel between the way the boys defer to their 'god' – the Lord of the Flies – and the way that they idolise Jack. He is, in a sense, lord over them – his own flies, or menials.

Simon's behaviour raises certain questions. In Chapter 1 it became evident that he is prone to fainting; in Chapter 9 it appears that he is epileptic: 'Simon's fit passed' (p. 160). His actions then may be governed by his medical condition and he is hallucinating. However, his understanding of the Lord of the Flies goes beyond that expressed in normal speech and thought, to an almost spiritual sympathy for the creature.

Simon emerges from the undergrowth and approaches the pig's head, communicating with it both verbally and with silent understanding. Back at the conch group camp, Ralph and Piggy discuss the fire as the thunder clouds gather. The importance of the fire to the boys' rescue is repeated. Ralph broaches the subject of what would happen if they gave up caring about rescue. Just as he is considering the central question of 'what makes things break up like they do?' (p. 154), his thoughts are disturbed by the arrival of the hunters.

Jack invites them to a feast, but this is simply a diversion to allow the raiders to steal some fire. Afterwards Ralph, Piggy, Sam and Eric and Bill consider Jack's offer and the lure of meat, but are not tempted to join the hunters.

Elsewhere, Simon is still communicating with the Lord of the Flies – the pig's head on a stick – which speaks to him in the voice of a school master. Eventually he falls unconscious.

CHECKPOINT 16

What does the voice of the schoolmaster represent?

Now take a break!

TEST YOURSELF (CHAPTERS 5–8)

WHO SAYS ...?

1 'We need an assembly. Not for fun. Not for laughing and falling off the log'

....

2 'I wanted – to go to a place – a place I know.'

....

3 'Daddy said they haven't found all the animals in the sea yet.'

....

4 'I don't believe in no ghosts – ever!'

....

5 'Who cares what you believe – Fatty!'

....

ABOUT WHOM?

6 Presently he stood up, holding the dripping sow's head in his hands.

....

7 He knew that one of his times was coming on. The Lord of the Flies was expanding like a balloon.

....

Check your answers on p. 84.

CHAPTER 9 – A View to a Death

❶ Simon climbs to the mountain top where he considers the corpse of the dead parachutist.

❷ Having worked out what it is, he makes his way down to tell the other boys.

❸ Below, the boys are indulging in tribal dances.

❹ Simon stumbles into the dancing circle.

❺ The boys kill Simon in their frenzy.

❻ The bodies of Simon and the parachutist are washed out to sea.

Simon is lying next to the Lord of the Flies. A storm is brewing, but nothing moves except the flies on the pig's head and intestines. Eventually Simon wakes from his fit, still intent, it seems, on climbing the mountain. His recent experience has left him weak and bloody, his eyes have lost their usual lustre. He staggers up the mountain against the gathering wind.

Arriving at the top, he finds the flyblown body of the parachutist. The suspension lines of the parachute create the impression that the body is moving. Simon examines the condition of the rotting corpse and is violently sick. He untangles the parachute lines so that the body is stilled and, observing the new camp the boys have apparently made on the beach, decides, despite his frailty, to return and tell them the news.

CHECKPOINT 17

In what way is Piggy parental?

Back at the bathing pool Ralph is enjoying the water – even Piggy ventures in. The heat is oppressive as the thunder clouds gather, giving Piggy a headache which makes him yearn for cool rain. The other boys have gone to Jack's camp, they believe. Piggy and Ralph decide to visit it to have some meat. Piggy again shows himself to be both parental and protective in his anxiety to visit Jack's camp 'to make sure nothing happens' (p. 163). What do you think he feared might occur? Could even Piggy have anticipated the outcome of the dance? Is it significant that, like Simon, Piggy has a headache just before these dramatic events happen?

Piggy and Ralph can hear the boys well before they see them. Jack is the focal point of the camp, surrounded by food and drink, bedecked with leaves and daubed in paint. The description of Jack's camp, in which he is set apart as being superior, is in marked contrast to the earlier assemblies with Ralph and the conch. Ralph's meetings were good-natured, inefficient and democratic. Jack's are severely businesslike, authoritarian and even dictatorial.

The babble of noise drops as the pair enter the camp. The silence is broken by laughter as two boys accidentally burn Piggy with hot meat. Jack dominates the whole group like an imperious monarch – offering meat, ordering drink and extending an invitation to join his tribe.

Jack and Ralph vie for leadership; one pressing the value of meat, the other the importance of shelters. The stalemate is broken as the rain starts and Jack suggests that the boys perform their dance. At first Roger plays the pig, then amid the rising frenzy and chanting he rejoins the hunters, leaving the centre of the circle empty. The littluns start a circle of their own but soon return to the biguns making a large, horseshoe shape. In the climax of chanting, dancing, thunder and lightning Simon emerges from the undergrowth with the news of the dead man on the hill. His words are ignored as the boys use him as the pig – the victim of their dance – and in the frenzy he is killed.

DID YOU KNOW?

Golding was a keen officer in his school's Cadet Corps. In 1943, to celebrate the honoured visit of a Russian colonel, the boys conducted fleet manoeuvres on the school field – mounted on bicycles!

CHECKPOINT 18

What fate do Simon and the parachutist share?

Images of light and dark, clear and opaque, are important throughout the book but are particularly strong in this chapter.

On the mountain top, the now-released parachute carries the body into the sea. As the rain stops the tide washes Simon's body out to sea as well. The stars in the night sky pick out strange, luminous creatures which surround Simon's body with light.

Simon – the martyr for the truth

Simon is determined to reach the top of the mountain where, in a sense, the truth lies – both literally and metaphorically. Simon frees the dead airman, who is then given the dignity of a burial at sea. Simon too is consigned to the sea after his murder. The news of 'a body on the hill' (p. 168) provides a clear piece of Christian imagery. Simon can be viewed as a prophet and visionary, with a parallel between the parachutist on the mountain and Christ on the hill at Calvary. The description of the halo of creatures which surround him with light as he floats out to sea is both poignant and significant. The fact that his news is ignored by the boys may also be worth some consideration.

DID YOU KNOW?

Golding was a devout Christian.

CHAPTER 10 – The Shell and the Glasses

1. Piggy and Ralph discuss the events of the previous night.
2. Jack and the hunters have set up camp on the rocky outcrop.
3. Ralph and Piggy try unsuccessfully to re-light the fire.
4. In an attack on Piggy, the hunters steal his glasses.

On the morning after Simon's death, Piggy squints at an approaching figure and recognises him as Ralph, who now looks as dishevelled as the rest of the boys. Without actually mentioning Simon, they slowly come round to the subject by discussing the need for an assembly. Ralph scoffs at the futility of the conch and talks about Simon and what he now realises was his murder. Piggy sees this admission as negative and unhelpful. He views Simon's death as the product of

GLOSSARY
imperious bossy

CHECKPOINT 19

How do Ralph and Piggy avoid their feelings of guilt for the death of Simon?

fear and 'that bloody dance' (p. 173) – eventually dismissing it as an accident which is best put out of their minds. Ralph and Piggy gradually convince themselves that they had nothing to do with it.

Sam and Eric return from collecting wood; they too deny being present at the feast – although they clearly were.

The camp now set up at Castle Rock is guarded by sentries who challenge Roger. He says he could still climb up to the rock if he wanted to, at which they show him a simple device to deter unwelcome visitors. (There is a lever pushed under the highest rock so that it can be dropped on enemies approaching along the narrow strip of land leading to the camp.) Roger admires the ingenuity of Jack, whom he regards as a 'proper Chief' (p. 176). Jack is apparently going to take them hunting. He is also going to punish Wilfred for some vague and undisclosed misdemeanour. Roger considers the consequences of ungoverned power.

The organisation of Jack's group is significant. Again he is placed in a prominent position with a semi-circle of boys around him. As on a previous occasion he is revered and set apart in importance. This contrasts sharply with the assemblies held using the conch, where everybody could speak and, like King Arthur's Round Table, everyone was of equal value. The semi-circle or horseshoe seems to invite someone or something to fill the opening it creates. It was into such a void that the hapless Simon stumbled on the previous evening.

Jack delivers instructions about the forthcoming hunt and the defence of Castle Rock. He proclaims that the beast – Simon – came in disguise the previous night. The muted suggestion that they killed Simon is emphatically denied by Jack. The beast might come again so they must leave the head of each kill as a gift to keep in favour with it. Their fire has gone out, so Jack plans to visit the other group with Maurice and Roger, keeping to the coastline to avoid the beast.

Ralph tries to relight the fire but the wood is too damp. Together with Piggy, Sam and Eric he contemplates methods of escape should the signal fire not attract rescuers. Eric considers the prospect of being 'taken prisoner by the reds' (p. 179) if they cannot get away, and suggests that this might be preferable to being captured by Jack and his savages. Ralph, tacitly admitting that he was a witness to the murder, reflects on Simon's last words about a dead man on the hill.

> **CHECKPOINT 20**
>
> How does Jack run his meetings?

Another attempt is made to light the fire which yet again proves unsuccessful. Sam and Eric, whether from shock or exhaustion, feel that their efforts are pointless, but Ralph reminds them that the fire is their only hope. However, because it is too dark to collect wood, they leave the fire to be lit the next day.

In the shelter Ralph casts his mind back to the security of home; he imagines the prospect of rescue and the lure and attraction of the civilised world. He drifts into a nightmare, from which Piggy awakens him. Sam and Eric too are troubled and fight together in their sleep. Ralph and Piggy recognise that the strain is affecting all of the boys.

Piggy hears a noise. Suddenly, his name is called and he believes, finally, that the beast is real after all and has come for him. The beast – Jack and his hunters – dives into the shelter and a fight ensues. Ralph pounds viciously into the face of an attacker until his efforts are halted by a knee in the groin, which fells him. There is **irony** in the misdirected aggression displayed by Ralph and Eric who, it turns out, were fighting each other in the darkness. Could this **symbolise** the pointlessness of violence used without thought or reason?

> **GLOSSARY**
> **reds** communists

When the perpetrators have gone the boys take stock of their injuries. Ironically Eric's face is bloody but he prides himself on the fact that he disabled his attacker by striking him between the legs! Piggy is uninjured, but is fearful for the safety of the conch. The hunters, meanwhile, return to Castle Rock – not with the conch but with Piggy's glasses.

This chapter describes the aftermath of Simon's murder. The tone is one of hopelessness and dejection among both the conch group and the savages of Castle Rock. Interestingly both groups, in one way or another, try to brush the incident aside by childishly-framed denials. Is it too far-fetched to suggest that the three-fold denial by the boys is an allegory for the biblical story of Simon Peter, who denied his knowledge of Christ on three occasions 'before the cock crows'? This aside, it is only Ralph who recognises the death for what it is – murder.

DID YOU KNOW?

The day when *Lord of the Flies* was published a zinc bath packed with ice and bottles of champagne appeared in the staff room at Golding's school.

It is useful at this point to reflect on what all the boys had experienced over their time on the island – fear, deprivation, discomfort, lack of parental care, illness, intimidation and depression. After all of these comes the heinous crime of murder – a crime of which they are all guilty, in a sense.

> ### The shell and the glasses
>
> The chapter is entitled 'The Shell and the Glasses', both of which are symbols. The shell could represent democracy, the voice of reason or decency (see **Law and order** in **Themes**). It is of no use in itself beyond being a beautiful object – its use is in what it represents or symbolises to the boys.
>
> The glasses are useful to Piggy, but have a function beyond that for everyone else – they can start the fire. The ability to make fire is something which sets human beings apart from animals. The glasses, therefore, symbolise fire, but also knowledge – enlightenment – and dominion over primitive instincts. It is notable that Piggy perceives the conch as the more valuable; holding it – literally – with respect and affection during the events of the next chapter.

CHAPTER 11 – Castle Rock

❶ Ralph is unable to light the fire.

❷ He and Piggy, with Sam and Eric, resolve to see Jack.

❸ A scuffle breaks out between the two groups.

❹ Piggy is killed by a falling rock.

❺ Ralph escapes alone.

Early next morning Ralph tries to salvage the beginnings of a fire from the previous day's ashes, but without Piggy's glasses his task is hopeless. As well as no fire, Piggy is virtually sightless without his glasses. He suggests that Ralph calls an assembly. Nobody turns up except Sam and Eric.

Ralph lists Jack's crimes – letting the fire go out, killing Simon, and now theft. When asked what he is going to do, Ralph suggests that they approach Jack as a civilised human being, not a savage, and explain the seriousness of being rescued.

Piggy, too, feels passionately that Jack should be told how to behave. Gaining his courage from the authority of the conch, he feels Jack should respond out of common decency and respect for the rule of law. Piggy conveys his faith in the ultimate power of the conch in the pride he exhibits at the prospect of carrying it to Castle Rock.

CHECKPOINT 21

What, says Piggy, is the one thing Jack hasn't got?

The boys consider tidying themselves up to remind the savages of the civilised world, but abandon the idea. They feel that however they look will be no worse than the appearance of the savages, who will be painted and masked – a thought which the twins find disconcerting. Ralph again repeats the need for smoke, although Piggy has to prompt him as to why it is so essential. Ralph resents the inference that he is losing his memory and reason, but Piggy is kindly and reassuring in support: 'You're Chief, Ralph. You remember everything' (p. 192).

The four boys walk in procession to Castle Rock, Piggy just able to glimpse the trailed butts of Sam and Eric's spears as they lead him, with Ralph at the rear. As Castle Rock comes into view, Ralph rearranges the order of the procession, putting himself in the lead, then Piggy followed by the twins. On the thin neck of land leading to the fort Piggy is concerned for his own safety because of his near blindness and the proximity of the cliff edge.

Ralph takes the conch and blows it. The savages appear. Roger behaves in a threatening manner; he has been left in charge while Jack is hunting. Ralph restates that he wants to call an assembly and, just as he is pressing his point about Piggy's glasses, Jack returns from a successful hunt.

Ralph charges Jack with the theft of the glasses. Indignant at the accusation, Jack stabs at Ralph who retaliates with righteous anger. The fight is halted with the boys trying to outface each other. Piggy, aware of his precarious position seated on the cliff, reminds Ralph of the reason for coming to Castle Rock. Ralph repeats the need for fire and is derogatory about the hunters' fire which is only suitable for cooking, and ineffectual as a signal.

CHECKPOINT 22

Do you think that the choice of Piggy's name is significant?

Piggy gains sufficient confidence from the fact that the boys are talking rather than fighting to stand up. At this point Jack orders his hunters to take the twins hostage. Sam and Eric – allied to Ralph – are easily captured and converted to become members of the tribe. Ralph, incensed by this further outrage, attacks Jack. Piggy effects a lull in the violence and, through the booing of the hunters and Roger's continued stone-throwing, chastises the boys for their behaviour. With the conch as his moral support, he repeatedly asks rhetorical questions about the choices they should make – 'Which is better, law and rescue, or hunting and breaking things up?' (p. 200). Whether from guilt at his questions, shame at their previous actions or recognition of Piggy as an enemy, the boys are outraged. Roger leans on the lever under the rock, tipping it down onto the approach path. Ralph sidesteps it but Piggy and the conch are struck. The conch is shattered and Piggy is knocked off the cliff and dies on a square rock forty feet below. Piggy has, quite literally, 'blind' faith in the power of the conch. It is significant that he dies at the same time that the conch – and all it **symbolises** – is destroyed.

Ralph is shocked but Jack, unrepentant, throws a spear which hits Ralph painfully in the chest – other spears follow. As Ralph makes his escape, Jack returns to the fort to interrogate Sam and Eric about their temerity in not joining his tribe.

The death of Piggy

There is a clear and unashamed parallel between the death of the pigs and the death of Piggy. Look at Piggy's demise – 'arms and legs twitched a bit, like a pig's after it has been killed' (p. 201) – and note the similarities between that and the graphic, earlier accounts of pig killings (in Chapter 8, for example).

The focus on Piggy as 'the centre of social derision' (p. 165) – a source of amusement – ends. Previously, the humour had been caused by slapstick (falling off the 'twister' log at the assembly), pantomime mimicry (Maurice pretending to be the pig) or at the Billy Bunter-like earnestness of Piggy ('the tribe were curious to hear what amusing thing he might have to say' [p. 199]). Schoolboy humour, or indeed fun of any sort, is not seen after this point.

Understandably in a novel featuring schoolboys, play – or 'Fun and games' (p. 223) – is a prominent form of behaviour. Play in nature is

CHECK THE BOOK

The spire in Golding's book of the same name belongs to Salisbury Cathedral, which was a hundred yards from where he taught.

often practice for something else – play-fighting prepares animals for hunting, for example. In human beings it may develop beyond the need for survival into more sophisticated social skills. Roger's stone-throwing, however, becomes dangerous and Jack's exaggerated dominance in the 'game' is now sinister.

CHAPTER 12 – Cry of the Hunters

❶ Ralph is now alone.

❷ He goes to speak to Sam and Eric at Castle Rock.

❸ The next morning, Jack and his group hunt him down.

❹ Isolated, Ralph collapses on the beach where he looks up to see the friendly face of a rescuing naval officer.

After escaping the hunters Ralph, bruised and bloody, reflects on his injuries and worries about whether the others are still pursuing him. He eventually comes out of hiding to spy on Castle Rock. The hunters are feasting and he decides that, for the moment at least, he is safe. He thinks about recent events and realises that Jack will not leave him in peace. He cannot fully come to terms with all that has happened. He eats some fruit and, understanding that he would not be safe in the shelter, walks on through the forest. He happens upon the remains of the pig's head; in fear and frustration he hits out at it and takes away the spear on which it is supported.

In the thicket near Castle Rock he rests but cannot sleep for fear of what might happen. He can hear the tribe dancing and see some savages keeping lookout, and regrets his isolation. Creeping towards the fort, he recognises the guards as Sam and Eric and awaits his chance to approach and speak to them.

CHECKPOINT 23

What might the pig's head now represent for Ralph?

Their manner is discouraging. They have been forced to join the tribe and they tell Ralph to go away for his own good. They also explain that Jack hates Ralph and plans to hunt him like a pig – the boys will sweep across the island in line to catch him, communicating with wavering cries.

Ralph fears, but cannot accept, what might happen to him. Sam and Eric are unhelpful beyond telling him to go and giving him some meat. He says that he is going to hide in the thicket which, being close to the fort, may be overlooked. The twins' parting remark is that Roger – now as terrifying as Jack – has 'sharpened a stick at both ends' (p. 211). Ralph fails to grasp the significance of this.

A little later, while tearing hungrily at the meat they had given him, Ralph hears angry voices and squeals of pain from the twins. He crawls hastily into the thicket and falls into a fitful sleep. He is woken in the morning by the cry of the hunters and creeps further into the dense thicket. By good fortune he finds a small space – created by the tumbling rock which killed Piggy – from which he can see the fort. Soon he can hear voices. The twins have been forced to give away his position. In the silence that follows, Ralph realises that one of the rocks on the cliff top is being levered to crash into the thicket. It misses him, despite the cheers of the savages at its fall.

> **CHECKPOINT 24**
> How can you tell that Ralph does not appreciate the danger he is in?

Again there is silence; this time another massive rock thunders through the thicket, knocking Ralph aside. Shaken but unhurt, he cowers in the undergrowth, striking out at one of the savages with his pointed stick. The unsuccessful attempts to dislodge Ralph lead the savages to try smoking him out. He heads out of the thicket towards the forest as the cries of the hunters sweep the island behind him.

Ralph realises that the signal means a hunter is unable to move forward because of the thickness of the undergrowth, and considers trying to break through the cordon. He also contemplates climbing a tree. His third option is to hide and wait for them to pass. In panic his mind seizes up, unable to think clearly without Piggy's help.

At last he decides to find somewhere to hide. Running past the pig's remains, he is aware that the forest is now on fire. He seeks out a dense, sunless thicket to hide in as the raging fire burns the fruit trees. As Ralph considers his fate, he spots a savage approaching with a stick 'sharpened at both ends' (p. 220). It is identical to his own and he understands its significance at last. After killing Piggy, Roger has become sadistic. In sharpening the stick at both ends – like the one used to impale the pig's head – he is obviously preparing to kill, and presumably behead, Ralph. As Sam and Eric pronounce, 'He's a terror' (p. 220).

CHECK THE BOOK

Golding drew on the tradition of adventure stories which he had loved as a boy. *Robinson Crusoe* (1719) was one of his favourites.

Ralph remains in place (Simon's statement that he would get back home reassuring him) until the tension is too great. Finally he breaks out and, dodging the spears, heads for the beach. He runs, almost numb and light-headed with terror and exhaustion, until he stumbles and falls on the sand.

Raising himself in expectation of the onslaught of the savages, he is faced by a naval officer, who has seen the smoke. He is alarmed by the boy's unkempt appearance and shocked that two boys have been killed on the island. As others emerge – including Jack – the officer expresses his surprise that British boys were not better able to survive. Ralph and other boys break down in relief at the end of their ordeal. The picture of Jack as a little boy belies the truth of his primitive, underlying aggression and savagery.

Rescued at last

Ralph has become an outcast, partly because he 'had some sense' (p. 206). He is alone now that Piggy and Simon are dead and Sam and Eric have been forced to change sides. Ralph's isolation, fear and pain are all described graphically. The atmosphere is tense and heightened by degrees to a climax.

The naval officer says that British boys should have 'put up a better show' (p. 224) and, he implies, not end up like savages. This is a **romanticised** view of their experience, as if they were characters from an adventure story like *The Coral Island*. The officer's enthusiasm echoes that of the boys in the first chapter and, in one sense, brings the story full circle. Yet, despite this, we are left with a lingering feeling of the darker realities of human nature.

Ralph's reaction at the end of the book is as much grief as relief. 'Ralph wept for the end of innocence, the darkness of man's heart, and the fall through the air of the true, wise friend called Piggy' (p. 225).

DID YOU KNOW?

Golding was in charge of the Sea Cadets when he taught in Salisbury.

Now take a break!

GLOSSARY
darkness evil

WHO SAYS ...?

1 'I got a pain in my head. I wish the air was cooler.'

....

2 'Piggy, come outside. I want you Piggy.'

....

3 'I got an awful bloody face, I think, Ralph. But I did him in the end.'

....

4 'We'll be like we were. We'll wash —'

....

5 'See? See? ... There isn't a tribe for you any more! The conch is gone —'

....

6 'You got to go, Ralph. You go away now —'

....

ABOUT WHOM?

7 'He's going to beat Wilfred.'

....

8 Still he did not move but lay there, his face sideways on the earth, his eyes looking dully before him.

....

9 He forgot his wounds, his hunger and thirst, and became fear; hopeless fear on flying feet

....

Check your answers on p. 84.

PART THREE

COMMENTARY

THEMES

Taken at face value, *Lord of the Flies* is a simple tale. Golding himself regarded it as a modern **fable** which can be enjoyed on more complex levels. One way to appreciate this is by exploring some of the themes of the book, to throw light on what William Golding wanted to say and on the times he was writing in. We discuss five themes below, but don't let this stop you finding and thinking about others of your own.

GOOD AND EVIL

The battle between good and evil is a central theme of *Lord of the Flies*. It appears in many conflicts – between the conch group and the savages, between the boys and the terrifying 'beast' and between rescue from a passing ship and imprisonment on the increasingly insane island, to name but a few.

Early in the novel, good is in the ascendancy. The conch provides a **symbol** of the decency and order of the society that the boys have come from (see **Law and order** below). Ralph organises the construction of shelters – mostly, in fact, the selfless work of himself and Simon – and a fire to signal to ships with. The boys spend the majority of their time playing and there are a few accidents, such as the fire that kills the birthmarked boy, but with Ralph's benign government, good is always dominant.

This situation is threatened as Jack continues his attempts to take over the conch group. He fails in this – a small victory for good – and sulks off to form his own 'tribe'. From then on, evil takes control. Boys join Jack's tribe because he hunts pigs and doesn't make them work. Ralph, representing the forces of good, is paralysed by indecision and has no effective response. Jack's tribe grows and his malevolence with it. Piggy's glasses are violently stolen, leaving him sightless. When the remainder of the conch group goes to retrieve the spectacles, Sam and Eric are captured and Piggy slain. Only the naval officer's intervention prevents the complete triumph of evil over good.

 CHECK THE NET
For some movie bloopers try **lordoftheflies.org/ blooper.htm**

Golding is giving us a warning about the power of evil, that if the good in people is not fostered then evil will take its place. The human urge to destroy will be unleashed and in the modern age there seem to be no limits to the harm this can do (see **Cold War paranoia** below). In this sense, *Lord of the Flies* can be seen as a cautionary tale, advocating change before it is too late.

LAW AND ORDER

The boys have come from a society in which orderliness is the norm and they attempt to continue this when they first arrive on the island.

DID YOU KNOW?

Golding thought the book showed a model civilisation destroyed from within.

Very quickly, the conch comes to **symbolise** values of this previous existence. The boys cannot talk at meetings unless they are holding the conch, and are thus forced to treat whoever is speaking with respect. This means that Piggy – in many ways a natural victim – is able to air intelligent thoughts that lead to improvements in the boys' lives. So toilets are moved away from the shelters and the boys try to keep a fire burning at all times. 'Parliaments' of this kind have always been key elements of successful civilisations, from Viking *tings* to our own system of government.

The other symbol associated with Piggy, his glasses, exposes a different side of law and order on the island. Rightfully they belong to Piggy, who needs them to see properly. Used with his permission, they also start the fires that are essential both to rescue and hygienically-cooked food. Jack – at school a figure of authority and order as head of the choir – refuses to respect Piggy's right to the glasses, first punching him and breaking a lens, then stealing the pair to start fires. In doing so, he challenges the law and order that have kept life on the island reasonable under Ralph. When the boys no longer accept law and order after this, Ralph is powerless and darker, more evil forces take over (see **Good and evil** above).

DISCIPLINE

William Golding was a teacher at Bishop Wordsworth's School for nine years before he wrote *Lord of the Flies*. In this time he grew unhappy with the English public school tradition that firm discipline was the best means of turning children into young adults.

The island is like a laboratory in which Golding can analyse the tensions that exist within a school. By removing the adults, he sets free the impulses and desires of the schoolboys and – almost – allows them to run their full course. So Jack, whom we presume to be arrogant and bullying at school, becomes first a wrecker of Ralph and Piggy's sensible plans, then a dictator, and finally a murderer. Piggy, on the other hand, is a permanent victim of Jack's bullying and is killed. Clearly these disasters could have been prevented by the normal orderliness of school life (see **Law and order** above).

Golding goes on to explore some of the problems that harsh discipline can conceal. A vivid demonstration is provided by the boys' sex lives. At first glance, sex is avoided in the book, not even getting the vague mentions that toiletry functions do. Looking closer, we find consistently sexual language used to describe the pig hunts and their re-enactments. For instance, 'Ralph too was fighting to get near, to get a handful of that brown, vulnerable flesh' (Ch. 7, p. 125). This comes to a head later in a hunt which almost reads like a gang rape, ending as the 'sow collapsed under them and they were heavy and fulfilled upon her' (Ch. 8, p. 149). Sex is taboo at school and continues the same on the island. So the boys' sexual urges come out in other ways, in particular in a desire to hurt the defenceless pigs. In the real world many serial killers and rapists share this inability to find sexual satisfaction in conventional and socially acceptable ways, and we see the results in the news every day.

DID YOU KNOW?

Golding loved playing chess.

Is Golding despairing of the school system he taught in? Not necessarily, for (as we saw in **Law and order**) Piggy's brains and Ralph's self-discipline result in positive achievements early in the novel, such as the fire and the shelters. And school discipline would restrict Jack's worst excesses. Difficulties only arise when this communal discipline is overwhelmed by the arbitrary discipline of a cruel leader – Jack – or immersed in the frenzy of a mob (see **Crowd mentality** below). What is needed is a balance between firm discipline and a certain creative freedom, and it is the absence of this that Golding is criticising in the schools of the time.

CROWD MENTALITY

At the start of the novel, we find a natural group already formed when Jack appears at the head of the choir. This group is disciplined, a fact which is of great help in hunting pigs, when good organisation is of paramount importance.

As order on the island breaks down (see **Law and order** above), the boys begin to behave differently when in groups. Pig hunts become ritualised and frenzied, marked by chants like, '*Kill the pig! Cut her throat! Kill the pig! Bash her in!*' (Ch. 4, p. 79). The boys act as a mob at these times and start to lose their individual identities. This absolves them of any direct blame for what happens and distracts them from their plight on the island.

DID YOU KNOW?

Golding's classroom in Salisbury gave him a good view of boys in the playground.

The climax of this crowd mentality comes when Simon returns with news that the 'beast' is actually a dead pilot. He stumbles into the midst of the near-hysterical savages during a night-time thunderstorm, and is himself taken to be the beast. The mob, including Ralph, 'leapt on to the beast, screamed, struck, bit, tore. There were no words, and no movements but the tearing of teeth and claws' (Ch. 9, p. 169). Afterwards Piggy and Ralph have great difficulty accepting that they have murdered Simon: '"It was an accident," said Piggy suddenly, "that's what it was. An accident."' (Ch. 10, p. 173).

In a mob, everyday life loses its meaning. Individuals are swallowed up and the mob seeks out those who are weak or simply outsiders to vent its fury on. There have been pogroms – where mobs kill members of minority groups – throughout history. Foremost in Golding's mind, however, when describing mob behaviour, was Nazi Germany. Jack in many ways echoes Hitler. At first charismatic and seeming to offer easy solutions to difficult situations, both learnt to use the fury of the mob against their enemies. Hitler turned mobs against Communists, Jews, homosexuals and, indeed, many of his own followers to eliminate opponents and terrify everyone else. Jack likewise kills and intimidates until complete control is almost in his hands. Witness particularly Eric's orders to hunt Ralph and throw his spear 'like at a pig' (Ch. 12, p. 209). Jack wants to use the pig-hunting mob frenzy to kill Ralph.

COLD WAR PARANOIA

The first use of atomic weapons in war – at Hiroshima in Japan on 6 August 1945 – undermined many people's assumptions about life.

Suddenly it seemed possible for the whole of civilisation to be destroyed by a single conflict.

This was not a practical problem until 1949, when the Soviet Union exploded its first A-bomb and the Cold War began in earnest. This was never an open war, although numerous conflicts, such as Korea, Vietnam and Afghanistan, were fought in its name. Rather it was an ideological battle in which anyone suspected of being the enemy would be attacked. Through the late Forties and early Fifties the infamous McCarthy witch-hunts were conducted in America. Many respected and influential people were destroyed by (often false) accusations that they were Communists. This paranoia – imagining that good, patriotic citizens were traitors – is deeply reminiscent of Jack and of Hitler's Germany (see **Crowd mentality** above).

In this context Golding wrote *Lord of the Flies*. A great deal of its stark confrontation – Jack against Ralph, savages against the conch group, even evil against good (see **Good and evil** above) – stems from the Cold War outlook. More specifically, the boys have been stranded by the Cold War turning into a real war. Their plane has presumably been shot down and the beast is a pilot who has ejected from his warplane.

On top of this, Golding was impressed by the Existentialist philosophy of writers such as Albert Camus, Jean-Paul Sartre and Samuel Beckett. Put simply, Existentialism claimed that God did not exist and that individuals were solely responsible for their own actions. So if you kill someone – as the savage mob does Simon – you must accept that you are responsible for your part of it, with no excuses. Ralph, as the force for good, tries to do this after Simon's death – 'That was murder' (Ch. 10, p. 172) – but even he fails.

Golding seems to be making several related points. Firstly he is saying that the world we know can be destroyed by atomic weapons. The island itself can be seen as a **metaphor** for the earth after a nuclear holocaust. Secondly, he is showing that the response to the Cold War – an hysterical and irrational desire to be on one side or the other, savage or conch – can only bring this nuclear disaster closer. Finally, he provides a way forward, through individuals taking responsibility for themselves and not being manipulated by the mob

CHECK THE BOOK

George Orwell's *Animal Farm* deals with a similar theme, where fairness and democracy are lost in a struggle for leadership.

mentality. If this had happened on the island, Piggy and Simon would both be alive when the naval officer arrives, and Ralph would probably still be chief, exercising his influence for good.

Instead society on the island breaks down, and we do have the deaths of Simon and Piggy. Golding is warning that a continuation of the Cold War, without a substantial increase in personal responsibility, will lead to the fate of the boys on the island for all humanity.

STRUCTURE

Lord of the Flies follows standard novel form with a simple and direct story-line. Although it is rightly regarded as a great piece of twentieth century literature by many people, it would be fair to say that it is limited – and deliberately so – in several obvious ways. For instance, the structure is dictated (as in any novel) by the characters and setting: Golding places his characters on an island, hence the events are largely a product of those people, their reactions and relationships as they engage with each other and that environment. Apart from the naval officer and ratings at the end and the parachutist halfway through, no one arrives on the island but the boys. And no one leaves – with the exception of the three who die, departing in a spiritual sense.

The boys, then, are placed in a vacuum; the story is moved along and structured by their social chemistry as it evolves in that restricted setting. That this works in so powerful and convincing a way, with such limiting and unlikely ingredients, seems a surprise. But, as Novalis – the German **Romantic** poet – suggested, 'Character is Fate'. The use of child characters, too, would appear unpromising, but the rivalry between Jack and Ralph – the result of their conflicting natures – together with their supporting cohorts, and Simon's **subplot** carries the story – but only in part.

Although no other living character visits the island during the boys' stay, the descent of the parachutist injects an important element into the structure of the action. The 'beast', in whatever shape – dead pilot, the 'fear', or as Simon, mistakenly killed in its place – provides another source of tension.

**CHECK
THE BOOK**
A number of other books are written from a child's perspective: *The Catcher in the Rye* (1951) and *Cider with Rosie* (1959) are two of the best!

These two strands of human conflict on one side and fear of the beast on the other grow as the story develops. This expansion is coupled with the gradual and simultaneous degeneration of morals and morale towards an inevitable – and perhaps anticipated – climax.

It is also worthwhile to consider the structure of the novel in terms of time and space, and as three distinct 'blocks' of action and development. All the events take place over a period of several weeks. How many is uncertain, but the passage of time is suggested by the loss of memory in one boy and Ralph's observation about the growth of the boys' hair. The first four chapters establish the characters and their behaviour; the middle section looks at the development of differences, exploring fears and obsessions; and the last four show the solution of those conflicts with death and finally, deliverance.

DID YOU KNOW?

Golding said his novels had a theatrical shape: building to a climax with a sudden fall at the end.

CHARACTERS

RALPH

Ralph is portrayed as the epitome of British boyhood – handsome, sporting, decent and honourable, but not possessed of any great intelligence or imagination. He is kindly – notice how, after Jack is defeated in the first election and Simon has just recovered from his faint, he chooses them to go exploring with him. Golding describes him as mild-featured: 'there was a mildness about his mouth and eyes that proclaimed no devil' (Ch. 1, p. 5). He has no hidden depth or unhealthy character traits.

Ralph's father is a commander in the Royal Navy and he has travelled fairly widely. His wish to return to the oft-described image of his middle-class home sustains him through his ordeal. His views on cleanliness are not typical for boys of his age! Again this is linked to his natural sense of decency. His disgust at the state of the boys is largely due to a comparison with what he sees as acceptable levels of hygiene and civilised behaviour.

Having a father in the Armed Forces may go some way to promoting a sense of order (**Law and order** in **Themes**) and appreciation for

Practical
Determined
Fair-minded
Athletic
Kind
Confident

DID YOU KNOW?

The names of the boys are similar to those in *The Coral Island* – deliberately so, according to Golding.

reasoned argument and systematic problem-solving. Ralph, after all, devises the convention that only the boy holding the conch is allowed to speak.

He possesses the confidence of his class, but little of its arrogance. Although he behaves with boyish superiority over Piggy when the boys arrive – even using his knowledge of the fat boy's nickname to raise a laugh – he lacks the malice of Jack. He appreciates Piggy's sense of humiliation over the matter and finds the way out, 'Better Piggy than Fatty ... I'm sorry if you feel like that' (Ch. 1, pp. 21–2). Despite recognising Piggy as an outsider he develops both respect and affection for him and his qualities.

Ralph exhibits a quiet authority that the boys appreciate and prefer to Jack's more strident and threatening manner. Ralph's leadership style and skills of oratory improve with experience. These, together with a perseverance on practical matters and confidence in his own ideology, lend weight to his suitability as chief.

However, it is not until he learns the ability to think more deeply and incisively that he is able to function effectively. Piggy's bequest, the ability to think (when pursued by the hunters), is ultimately responsible for his survival.

At the end of the book, it is he who has the insight to sum up the lost opportunities of the island: 'he wept for the end of innocence ... and the fall through the air of the true, wise friend called Piggy.' (Ch. 12, p. 225)

PIGGY

Piggy's unprepossessing appearance and isolation prevent him from making a full contribution to life on the island. Even Ralph is dismissive of him at first, regarding him, perhaps correctly, as a whining and overweight hypochondriac who can be ordered about. Piggy is the boy who would be chosen last for the football team. He seems to have little to commend him when survival on a desert island is at stake.

He is set apart in other ways too. His background is plainly working class, not middle class like Ralph, Jack and the choir. Presumably he is a scholarship boy. As Ralph observes, 'Piggy was an outsider, not only by accent, which did not matter, but by fat, and ass-mar, and specs, and a certain disinclination for manual labour' (Ch. 4, p. 68). He is socially unacceptable and somewhat inept. He fears people, possibly because of his experience of past treatment and cruelty.

Yet, for all this, he is probably the most intelligent boy on the island. He has the foresight and good sense of an older person; he exhibits a degree of caution and some organising ability. He puts his finger on the cause of the trouble amongst the boys, 'them that haven't no common sense' (Ch. 8, p. 145) he terms them. He displays moral and physical courage in upholding the supremacy of the conch but most important of all, he is a thinker.

It is his ability to think which he passes to Ralph. When Jack says Piggy and Ralph are alike he means in the sense that they are thoughtful and serious-minded, rather than in any physical way. Piggy is not only imaginative but can solve problems using lateral and/or rational thought. When he addresses the problem of making an easily-tended fire with sufficient smoke to attract ships or aeroplanes, he suggests: We could 'experiment. We could find out how to make a small hot fire and then put green branches on to make smoke' (Ch. 8, p. 143). Even if his courage fails him in practice, he is logical in his treatment of the theory. He is protective of his rights and, like Ralph, fair-minded and egalitarian.

His intelligence is the natural complement to Ralph's common sense. Their relationship is symbiotic – each supports the other – like Don Quixote and Sancho Panza in Cervantes's famous novel, or, more appropriately, Robinson Crusoe and Man Friday. They are more influential and effective when working together, each possessing qualities that the other lacks.

JACK MERRIDEW

Jack is a character Golding has clearly intended you dislike. He provides little basis for empathy in either his words or his actions. Even from his dramatic entrance – the procession of capped and gowned choirboys along the beach, in itself anachronistic and sinister – he is arrogant and aggravating. He is completely in charge of his

Intelligent
Asthmatic
Wears glasses
Overweight
Working class

 CHECK THE FILM

Hugh Edwards, who played Piggy in the 1963 film, was the only boy from England.

Arrogant
Pugnacious
Envious
Dictatorial
Hunter

choir and Ralph immediately recognises that he has 'the voice of one who knew his own mind' (Ch. 1, p. 17).

He assumes leadership on the basis that he is chapter chorister, can sing C sharp and is head boy – none of which necessarily fit him for high office on a desert island, except possibly the last. Being head boy only means that he is familiar with the task of leadership, not that he is automatically skilled at it. In many respects the opposite is true, as we discover.

His main contribution to the survival of the boys is to track the pigs and provide meat. For him it becomes a 'compulsion to track down and kill that was swallowing him up' (Ch. 3, p. 51). Meat is not absolutely essential to their survival (the island has fruit, crabs and shellfish as well) yet he insists on its importance. In this sense he represents Man the Hunter; although he sees the whole experience on the island as a game, he exhibits a basic, primeval instinct – the urge to hunt.

Unfortunately, his simplistic and single-minded approach is self-destructive and lacking in foresight. Two examples illustrate this: the boys kill a sow, which could have bred and provided future meat; and, in their hunt for Ralph, they destroy the fruit trees. These two over-hasty actions mean that they would eventually have starved.

The other consequence of Jack's hunting instinct is bizarre and sinister. He goes from hunting animals to hunting people. When Simon stumbles down from the mountain with the truth about the beast, it is Jack with his orders, 'Do our dance! Come on! Dance!' (Ch. 9, p. 167) who sets in motion the sequence of events that will lead to his death. Survival then becomes not a matter of finding food but manifests itself in warfare. He uses the weapons and skills developed from necessity to enforce his will (see **Crowd mentality** in **Themes**).

Although Jack's personality traits make him what he is, background and conditioning, it could be argued, are also contributory factors. On the one hand he has the archetypal, red-haired temper, together with a natural dominance. On the other, his training in a very middle-class, religious and ritualistic school environment is reflected in the behaviour and actions of his tribe. They wear strange garments, sing and chant and administer seemingly arbitrary punishments.

Jack's physical appearance throughout the novel is also a deliberate and blatant warning sign. His red hair stands out. As well as being associated with a fiery temper it also, significantly, indicates danger. When he, quite literally, masks his appearance with paint, far from neutralising his venom and pugnacity it gives it free rein. When he is 'safe from shame or self-consciousness behind the mask of his paint' (Ch. 8, p. 154) he can act as he wishes and realise his most extreme and evil potential (see **Good and evil** in **Themes**).

Jack's lack of humility, along with his bravado and dictatorial leadership are all intended to conflict with the ideals Golding creates in some of his other characters. Jack's final appearance in Chapter 12 portrays him as a little boy, perhaps re-emphasising how thin the veneer of conditioning and respectability can be when set against the primal instincts shown in his earlier actions.

SIMON

Simon exhibits a number of contradictory characteristics. He is helpful and community-spirited – helping with the shelters – yet is, on occasions, reclusive and solitary. He is, as Ralph says, 'always about' (Ch. 3, p. 56) but spends time alone in the forest. Although he is shy and timid during the assemblies – not being able to bring himself to speak his deepest thoughts honestly – he shows great courage in other respects; he walks alone through the jungle at night and even climbs the mountain to face the beast.

Kind
Sensitive
Introvert
Perceptive
'Spiritual'

He is described on numerous occasions as 'batty', 'queer', 'funny' and 'crackers', but quite what form this strangeness takes is never really explicit. The boys lack the vocabulary to define and so pigeon-hole him as a particular type. He is evidently kind and considerate to others – helping the littluns and showing concern for Piggy. He is thought of as odd principally because he is different.

None of the other boys, with perhaps the exception of Piggy, has anything like his insight. It is Simon who tries to explain the notion of evil which manifests itself in 'the fear' and 'the beast', by asking, 'What's the dirtiest thing there is?' (Ch. 5, p. 96). He has the intellect and maturity to understand the concept, but lacks the language to express it. We can only assume that his perception has been regarded as strange and alien on other occasions – in part accounting for his strangeness – which is why he is reluctant to voice his feelings with confidence.

Despite saying comparatively little in the book, it is often Simon who captures moments of potential enlightenment in a single sentence. He assures Ralph, for example, that he will get back home and puts into words Ralph's wonderment at the immensity of the sea. It is Simon who feels the need to go up the mountain to see the beast for what it is but his insistence is, once again, ignored. He shows determination in discovering the truth for himself, but is killed by the boys before he can share his knowledge with them.

DID YOU KNOW?

Golding enjoyed eating candyfloss, despite the fact that it clogged up his beard!

He has considerable strength of mind but is frail of body, and enters the story fainting, something he appears to do regularly. He seems to suffer from epilepsy or some similar condition. Simon is often regarded as a prophet – even a saint or Christ figure – and there are certainly images to support such a view. When he understands the nature of the beast and the significance of this for the boys, 'that it is harmless and horrible' (Ch. 9, p. 162) and that it proves there is life outside the island, his concern for others takes him down into the tribal dance where he is to die. His perception and individuality, combined with his human vulnerability make him an intriguing character, however you see him.

ROGER

Sadistic

Jack's lieutenant

The degeneration from man to animal, from red-cheeked choirboy to premeditated killer, can be seen most obviously in Roger. He is Jack's lieutenant, and it is significant that it is to Roger that Jack shows the clay which they later use for their masks. Roger is Jack's partner in crime but ultimately outstrips even him in barbarism. He has, from the start, a sadistic streak, teasing Henry in the stone-throwing incident. Most significantly, it is Roger who 'with delirious abandonment' (Ch. 11, p. 200) levers the rock forty feet down on to Piggy's head. As the final hunt on Ralph gets under way, it comes as no surprise to us that a stick Roger sharpened 'at both ends' (Ch. 12, p. 211) in preparation for the hunting of Ralph; its use is clear and horrifying to us, although Ralph finds it difficult to comprehend.

SAM AND ERIC

Interestingly, Sam and Eric do not join Jack's tribe at first and only finally do so when forced. Perhaps, behaving as one person they are strong enough or sufficiently secure in themselves not to be influenced by Jack. Whatever the reason, they become, and remain for much of the novel, Ralph's 'tribe'. They are treated as one person, even when taking a shift at the fire. Like many twins they have their own understanding of a private language and finish each other's sentences.

It is not until the night of the raid that they disagree and fight with each other in their sleep. When Sam says that he got 'mixed up with myself' (Ch. 10, p. 185) does he mean that he literally got tangled up or is he fighting with his other self – his twin? This might be interpreted as depicting a human being in a dilemma, good and evil fighting within him (see **Good and evil** in **Themes**).

MAURICE

In much the same way that Roger is next in command to Jack, Maurice is Roger's henchman. However, whereas Roger goes on to become 'a terror' (Ch. 12, p. 210), Maurice retains much of his original sense of sin and a natural reserve. After the incident on the beach with the littluns, he feels guilty in a way that Roger does not. Throughout the novel Maurice, although a loyal savage, remains stolid and unimaginative.

ROBERT

Robert is further down the pecking order of the savages than Maurice but, unlike him, is a natural 'follower'. He fits comfortably into their life and activities. It is Robert, together with Maurice, who skewers the pig's head on a stick and enters into the pantomime version of pig-killing which is the precursor of the event which leads to Simon's death.

PERCIVAL WEMYS MADISON

Percival's name is supposed to indicate a very middle-class background. Even early on his conditioned response begins to dwindle, 'Percival Wemys Madison, The Vicarage, Harcourt St. Anthony, Hants, telephone, telephone, tele—' (Ch. 5, p. 93). By the end of the novel, 'Percival Wemys Madison sought in his head for an incantation that had faded clean away' (Ch. 12, p. 224). The influences of his home life and background are made to look thin and superficial alongside the starker reality of his experiences on the island.

THE BOY WITH THE BIRTHMARK

Throughout the novel the littluns remain largely anonymous; Golding deliberately gives this little boy a physical characteristic which makes him memorable. Hence, when he is missing after the over-zealous fire-lighting on the mountain, it is obvious that he has disappeared and the boys are made strongly aware of the consequences of their actions.

THE PARACHUTIST

Having asked for a sign from the outside world, the dead airman is not, perhaps, what the boys had in mind. It is interesting that none of them sees him for what he is – a dead human being – but rather as a representation of defeat, death and decay. He is also the manifestation of evil and the boys' worst fears in the form of 'the beast'. Only Simon gets close to recognising the reality and facts of the matter, treating him with dignity and compassion.

CHECK THE FILM
A second version was made in 1990 by Harry Hook. It includes additional characters who are not in the novel and is, therefore, less helpful for students of the text.

THE NAVAL OFFICER

In contrast with the dead airman, the naval officer offers a sanitised view of the war and Service life. In his white, Tropical kit he appears like a knight in shining armour; the cavalry – a final cliché – offering the boys deliverance. He is clearly shocked that British boys could not 'put up a better show' (Ch. 12, p. 224) when he is told about the deaths and possesses a rather romantic notion of what life must have been like for them. His arrival echoes Ralph's idea that his father, 'a commander in the Navy' (Ch. 1, p. 8), would eventually rescue them. There is **irony** in the fact that they are being returned to the same war which caused the demise of the parachutist – a 'war' no less brutal than that which afflicted all the boys on the island.

LANGUAGE AND STYLE

When a writer has conceived a plot, developed characters, considered themes and related issues – all that is contained in the initial creative process – only then can the craft begin. Because his or her medium is the written word and the intention to communicate to an unseen reader in a common language, on the basis of little shared experience or identity, linguistic choices are, to say the least, difficult! A bewildering array of devices, a clutter of vocabulary and an armoury of figures of speech are at the author's disposal. Although writers use these deliberately to create effect, they can use them with an ease and precision that does not appear contrived or clumsy. It is this that shows the writer's craft, and this that we, as teachers and students, point to and admire.

A MODERN FABLE

Golding intended to convey a number of messages in his 'modern fable', none of which were light-hearted or flippant. His pessimism about the natural state of human beings – their culpability and sinfulness – and his own cynicism about life inevitably inform the style and tone of his writing. None of this is trivial; his tone is one of hopelessness and despondency at the inevitability of evil and unpleasant things happening. Yet he does not overstate the more morbid perspective, nor does he become maudlin. He shows us plainly what the consequences might be, then leaves us to think and to learn.

What Golding has to teach us is delivered objectively, without apparent bias. In passages of description, we are told what is happening with the faithfulness of a neutral observer; indeed, we must sometimes search hard for meanings. In sections of dialogue, exchanges are pithy and direct but the nuances of speech and action are related without prejudice, so we may draw our own conclusions.

DID YOU KNOW?

Golding was not happy that the book was made into a film in 1963. He preferred working inside the head of a reader.

Scrutiny of some of the descriptive prose passages reveals that Golding uses a wide range of literary devices and figures of speech. Pages 58–61 are a rewarding point at which to start looking for this. *Lord of the Flies* contains examples of **allegory**; similes and **metaphors** abound, together with **hypallage, irony**, slang, **symbolism** and **imagery**.

IRONY

Golding's use of irony is both interesting and highly relevant to the tone and message of the novel. In terms of style, irony provides a powerful vehicle for some (often quite macabre) statements about life and fate. Irony is somewhat easier to illustrate than define; the following points may help you understand it:

EXAMINER'S SECRET

If you are going to use literary terms like 'irony', make sure you understand what they mean!

- Piggy is angry about the forest fire and the disappearance of the boy with the birthmark – but Piggy's glasses were used to start the fire, so he is indirectly responsible.

- Simon returns to the camp with the truth about the beast, which could dispel the boys' fears. He is killed before he can tell his news.

- After the raid, Ralph and Eric feel proud of how well they fought. They were, in fact, fighting each other in the darkness.

- The rock which kills Piggy clears a space in the thicket – enabling Ralph to escape the hunters and so survive.

- Jack's hunters set fire to the bushes to smoke out and kill Ralph. It is this fire which draws attention to the island and effects the boys' rescue.

- The boys are taken away from the 'war' on the island by a naval officer who is involved in, and returning them to, another war.

It can be seen then that irony is a type of reversal of ideas, and shows how seemingly good events often lead to bad – and vice versa.

DIALOGUE

In contrast with the complexity of the descriptive pieces, the sections of dialogue are terse and almost monosyllabic. The best way for you to see this is by studying some short sections in detail yourself. The boys rarely speak more than a few sentences at a time; often their utterances amount to just a few words and their vocabulary – for boys who are quite well educated – is limited. (Try counting the number of words, syllables and sentences in a typical section of speech in any chapter.) They also resort to boyish slang and mild swearing; their exclamations mirror those of cartoon or comic characters and they lack some of the vocabulary needed to discuss more sophisticated concepts.

SYMBOLISM

Lord of the Flies can be viewed as like an onion – it has a simple story-line with ever increasing 'rings' of meaning around that central core. As a **fable** it is uncomplicated, but the surrounding 'rings' cover many deeper issues. The story contains, for instance, a number of **symbolic** objects. The conch is more than just a shell, useful for attracting attention and summoning the boys to meetings. It is like a church bell calling the faithful, and embodies some of the ritual of religious ceremonies. For the boys on the island it also imposes a sense of order (see **Law and order** in **Themes**). Only one person can hold the conch, so only one person can speak at a time and, unlike Jack's assemblies, everyone is given that right. The conch can, therefore, symbolise free speech, democracy, order and unity.

Piggy's glasses are more than an aid to his poor eyesight. To the boys the glasses symbolise fire – without which, as Ralph repeatedly proclaims, they cannot be rescued or cook the meat which Jack provides. Fire then is representative of life, but sadly and **ironically**, it is also the element which causes the death of the boy with the birthmark and very nearly leads Ralph to the same fate. By association, the glasses symbolise life (and death), knowledge, power and dominance.

The beast, whether real or imaginary, is symbolic. It represents what Ralph calls 'the darkness of man's heart' (Ch. 12, p. 224). This is the 'beast' present in each of us – the capacity for evil and wrongdoing (see **Good and evil** in **Themes**). This beast must be served and accommodated and so the Lord of the Flies (the pig's head on a stick) becomes its shrine. The boys' recognition of evil, or the Devil, is embodied in the sacrifice they make after each kill.

 CHECK THE FILM

The first film version was by Peter Brook in 1963.

The pig's head symbolises all of this to Simon, and also the cynicism of adults and the hollowness and superficiality of their world. It is Simon who sees the parachutist as epitomising the capacity of adults for death and destruction. He symbolically frees this when he releases the suspension lines of the parachute.

Although symbolism is, in part, tied to objects, it may be seen here that actions can also be symbolic. Think, for example, of the hunters baptising themselves with the blood of the pig, or the death of the sow representing the boys relinquishing a mother figure – and so, parental ties and innocence.

IMAGERY

Images are 'pictures' which reflect (and so **symbolise**) something else. These pictures can be in the form of simple similes and **metaphors,** which allow us to better imagine an incident or scene by drawing on our own experience. For example, think about expressions such as 'like raindrops on a wire' or 'like an angry eye' (Ch. 4, p. 60). Or consider the metaphorical use of language: 'a bowl of heat and light' (Ch. 3, p. 58) and 'darkness poured out' (Ch. 3, p. 59). Beyond these are more complex pictures which demand more involved parallels to be drawn.

Most readers will be able to empathise with images like light and dark, hot and cold or clear and opaque. The contrasts of positive and negative, (and therefore good and bad) are obvious and unashamed.

Images are often themed in the novel. Simon is linked to natural images; and images of death are often encountered where Jack is present. Ralph contemplates the sea, another natural image. Simon is prophet-like in many ways, including his withdrawal to the jungle to meditate. He is seen being 'tempted' by the Lord of the Flies; haloed in light when he dies; bringing a 'truth' which nobody listens to; freeing the dead airman from, quite literal, corruption and expressing spiritual understanding. Other images are rewarding if we take particular notice of Simon in this context.

DID YOU KNOW?

Lord of the Flies was the first of Golding's thirteen novels.

PART FOUR

RESOURCES

HOW TO USE QUOTATIONS

One of the secrets of success in writing essays is the way you use quotations. There are five basic principles:

EXAMINER'S SECRET
When studying/ revising, identify some key quotations which may be used for a variety of possible essays.

❶ Put inverted commas at the beginning and end of the quotation.

❷ Write the quotation exactly as it appears in the original.

❸ Do not use a quotation that repeats what you have just written.

❹ Use the quotation so that it fits into your sentence.

❺ Keep the quotation as short as possible.

Quotations should be used to develop the line of thought in your essays. Your comment should not duplicate what is in your quotation. For example:

> **Jack thinks he should be chief automatically because he is head boy, 'I'm chapter chorister and head boy. I can sing C sharp'.**

Far more effective is to write:

> **Jack thinks he should be chief automatically because he is, 'chapter chorister and head boy'.**

However, the most sophisticated way of using the writer's words is to embed them into your sentence:

> **Ralph thought that Simon was fun-loving because his eyes were 'delightfully gay and wicked', which was partly true.**

When you use quotations in this way, you are demonstating the ability to use text as evidence to support your ideas – not simply including words from the original to prove you have read it.

COURSEWORK ESSAY

Set aside an hour or so at the start of your work to plan what you have to do.

- List all the points you feel are needed to cover the task. Collect page references of information and quotations that will support what you have to say. A helpful tool is the highlighter pen: this saves painstaking copying and enables you to target precisely what you want to use.

- Focus on what you consider to be the main points of the essay. Try to sum up your argument in a single sentence, which could be the closing sentence of your essay. Depending on the essay title, it could be a statement about a character: Ralph is the character Golding intended his readers to admire most, but he could have survived better if Piggy had lived; an opinion about setting: Golding chose the island to show that 'no man is an island entire of himself' – human beings need other people, social order and a breadth of experience to survive. They cannot do so alone; or a judgement on a theme: The main theme appears to be that all human beings possess a sense of evil, to some degree.

- Make a short essay plan. Use the first paragraph to introduce the argument you wish to make. In the following paragraphs develop this argument with details, examples and other possible points of view. Sum up your argument in the last paragraph. Check you have answered the question.

- Write the essay, remembering all the time the central point you are making.

- On completion, go back over what you have written to eliminate careless errors and improve expression. Read it aloud to yourself, or, if you are feeling more confident, to relative or friend.

If you can, try to type you essay, using a word processor. This will allow you to correct and improve your writing without spoiling its appearance.

CHECK THE NET

Visit the official website of the Nobel foundation and find its notes on the book: **www. nobel.se/literature/ educational/ golding/**

SITTING THE EXAMINATION

Examination papers are carefully designed to give you the opportunity to do your best. Follow these handy hints for exam success:

BEFORE YOU START

- Make sure you know the subject of the examination so that you are properly prepared and equipped.

- You need to be comfortable and free from distractions. Inform the invigilator if anything is off-putting, e.g. a shaky desk.

- Read the instructions, or rubric, on the front of the examination paper. You should know by now what you have to do but check to reassure yourself.

- Observe the time allocation – and follow it carefully. If they recommend 60 minutes for Question 1 and 30 minutes for Question 2, it is because Question 1 carries twice as many marks.

- Consider the mark allocation. You should write a longer response for 4 marks than for 2 marks.

WRITING YOUR RESPONSES

- Use the questions to structure your response, e.g. question: 'The endings of X's poems are always particularly significant. Explain their importance with reference to two poems.' The first part of your answer will describe the ending of the first poem; the second part will look at the ending of the second poem; the third part will be an explanation of the significance of the two endings.

- Write a brief draft outline of your response.

- A typical 30-minute examination essay is probably between 400 and 600 words in length.

- Keep your writing legible and easy to read, using paragraphs to show the structure of your answers.

- Spend a couple of minutes afterwards quickly checking for obvious errors.

EXAMINER'S SECRET

If you cannot choose between two questions, jot down a plan for each to help you decide – it may be that what appeared to be the most straightforward question is more difficult than you thought.

EXAMINER'S SECRET

To do well, you do not have to write at great length: you can get the highest marks with an essay of two sides.

EXAMINER'S SECRET

Always turn over and check that there are no questions on the other side of the question paper or on the back page of the question book.

WHEN YOU HAVE FINISHED

- Don't be downhearted – if you found the examination difficult, it is probably because you really worked at the questions. Let's face it, they are not meant to be easy!

- Don't pay too much attention to what your friends have to say about the paper. Everyone's experience is different and no two people ever give the same answers.

IMPROVE YOUR GRADE

You have spent some time studying *Lord of the Flies* and, with the help of these York Notes, you have a good understanding of the novel. Coursework essays and examination questions give you an opportunity to show your knowledge – they are not meant to catch you out or make you look silly. By following some simple guidelines you will be able to write with confidence and easily improve your grade. The advice comes next will help you answer examination questions but may also be useful with other types of writing about the novel.

Your potential grades in any examination can be improved. Your paper is marked according to a marking scheme applied to all candidates and no examiner knows in advance your level of achievement. All candidates start with a blank answer booklet.

The commonest problem is a simple one: failure to answer the question. Do not begin writing until you know precisely what you want to say. Otherwise, it is far too easy to go off the point and start waffling. A good idea is to look back occasionally to the question and check that you are still answering it.

Keep an eye on the clock. You will probably have two hours to answer two questions. Each is worth the same number of marks, so divide your time equally between them. Avoid the temptation to write at length on your preferred question and submit a skimpy response to the second.

One final point concerns the length of your answers. Your answer booklet is considered to be more than enough for the very best students to obtain the very best marks. There should be no need for you to request extra sheets unless your handwriting is extraordinarily large. If you are asking for extra paper, the chances are that a fair part of what you are writing is unnecessary.

IMPROVING YOUR GRADE FROM A D TO A C

- Remember that the first thing you write will be the first thing the examiner reads. Think carefully about your opening sentence. You need to make a good impression at the start. If you begin with

     I am going to look at the characters of Ralph and Jack ...

  this just states the obvious. (The examiner can see which question you have chosen by the number in the margin.) Instead, go in more directly with something like:

     Jack and Ralph are both complex and interesting characters and each in his own way contributes importantly to the storyline and outcome of the novel.

  This will have more impact and leave the examiner thinking that you are knowledgeable and confident about the subject. You should take just as much care with the concluding paragraph.

- Follow your plan. Make small sub-headings to help you with the paragraphing and structure of your writing. For example, if you were asked to compare the characters of Jack and Ralph, you might make notes under headings such as: Appearance, Behaviour, Relationships, Language, Character (what you like and dislike about them) and Importance (how important they are to the story).

- A lower-grade candidate will often just re-tell the story: resist the temptation to do this! If the examination question asks you to follow a character's progress, you must include some of your own comments and ideas. The examiner knows the story already, simply telling them what happened will not get you a good mark.

- A C-grade candidate will back up what s/he writes with evidence from the novel. Quotations are the most common and effective way of doing this – they show that you have a good knowledge of

EXAMINER'S SECRET

The good candidate refers to William Golding as 'Golding'
The average candidate will call him, 'William Golding'
The weak candidate just calls him 'William'!

the text and help you to prove your point. Never introduce a quotation by saying 'and I quote'; instead make your statement, add the quotation, then follow up to develop your point, like this:

Jack is a dominant and aggressive character. This is shown repeatedly in his treatment of Piggy: 'You're talking too much ... Shut up, Fatty.' He also takes Piggy's glasses away and is, in part, responsible for his death.

You might include about six to eight quotations in an examination answer.

IMPROVING YOUR GRADE FROM A B TO AN A

- To achieve an A grade, your answer must show a high level of understanding. You must show that you not only know the novel very well but are also capable of 'reading between the lines' – that is interpreting what you have read and drawing your own conclusions. Do not be afraid to give your own views on characters, themes and ideas - but always draw on evidence from the text to support what you say. Embedding quotations in your own sentences is the best way of doing this (see **How to use quotations**).

- Remember that this is an English examination so the English language is important. An A-grade candidate will consider ways in which the language has been used to good effect – even if the question does not make a direct reference to it. Ask yourself these questions: Has Golding used any special ways to give the language more impact? Has s/he used alliteration, **imagery**, **symbolism**, **metaphors** or similes to get his message across? Do different characters speak in different ways? Notice the difference between how Jack and Piggy speak, for example.

- Any literature tends to reflect something about the time and culture in which it was written. Golding was an English man and a schoolteacher who had experienced the Second World War and was disturbed by the atom bombs being dropped on Japan. All of these aspects of Golding's time and culture show up in the novel. An A-grade candidate will be aware of this and refer to the background of the novel where relevant.

EXAMINER'S SECRET

You must write on what the question asks, not on what you feel like writing.

- *Lord of the Flies* is more than just a good story; it also teaches us something about human nature. It has messages and morals from which we can learn. For example, we can see how humans behave in a primitive way, how they can be cruel, that they are easily influenced and can be bullied. What messages came across to you while reading the book? Include some of these in your answer, if possible – it will help to boost your grade.

Focus carefully upon the question set and plan your argument. Select quotations that accurately and relevantly support the points you wish to make. Higher-grade answers are achieved when you give a personal response that develops a line of thought, showing understanding of the techniques used by the author to affect your response.

When you have finished writing, you have one final and vital task: check what you have written. This is probably the worst part of the examination and no one likes reading what they have written. You have been working under pressure for the best part of two hours and you have almost certainly made careless errors. Now is the chance to correct them and send your paper on its way into the examination system, having given it the best possible chance!

EXAMINER'S SECRET

In an examination there is no difference between being asked to argue and being asked to persuade!

SAMPLE ESSAY PLAN

A typical essay question on *Lord of the Flies* is followed by a sample essay plan in note form. This does not present the only answer to the question, merely one answer. Do not be afraid to include your own ideas, and leave out some of those in the sample! Remember that quotations are essential to prove and illustrate the points you make.

Show how the sense of order on the island deteriorates over the course of the novel.

INTRODUCTION

William Golding wanted to explore the fragility of our civilisation. So, in *Lord of the Flies*, he abandons a group of schoolboys on a desert island and chronicles the battle between order and chaos that follows.

PART 1 – THE ESTABLISHMENT OF ORDER

- Ralph uses the conch to assemble the boys in one place.
- Jack, the head boy, feels he should be chief. When a democratic vote is held, however, Ralph wins comfortably.
- The conch becomes a symbol of the order of the world the boys have come from. To speak at a meeting one must hold the conch.
- Ralph points out that a fire is essential for signalling to ships, and so being rescued. A great fire is built on the mountainside.
- The fire rages out of control and the boy with the birthmark vanishes. Presumably he has burnt to death. Despite the boys' good intentions, they are still immature and a danger to themselves.

PART 2 – PAPERING OVER THE CRACKS

- The beast is discussed at a meeting, unsettling all of the boys.
- Ralph proceeds with his programme of improvements, helped by Piggy's intelligent suggestions. Shelters are built.
- Jack becomes obsessed with hunting.
- When the choir is meant to be tending the fire, Jack leads it on a hunt. The fire goes out and a ship passes by. Ralph is furious. Jack cannot challenge him but lashes out at Piggy – Ralph's brains – instead, breaking his glasses.
- Piggy's glasses are a symbol of order. Breaking them undermines order on the island.
- Ralph attempts to reassert his authority at a meeting. He says that the fire is of paramount importance.
- Fear of the beast persists. A hunt – Jack's area of expertise – is organised to kill it. Finding the parachutist moving in the wind, the boys are terrified. They decide that the beast is real and avoid it.

EXAMINER'S SECRET

Always write a plan for every answer.

PART 3 – THE COLLAPSE OF ORDER

- Jack challenges Ralph once more.
- Beaten a second time, Jack leaves to form his own 'tribe'.
- Tempted by hunting and feasting and not having to work, many boys join Jack's savages.
- The conch group continues to stand for order and fairness; the savages become a dark, erratic force.
- Simon – bearing the truth about the beast – is killed by the frenzied savage mob.
- Piggy's glasses are stolen. When the conch group attempts to retrieve them, Piggy is killed and Sam and Eric are forced to join the savages.
- Ralph, now alone, is hunted like a pig. He is no longer treated as a human. Only the naval officer prevents Ralph's death and the complete collapse of order.

CONCLUSION

At first, the boys try to replicate the orderly environment they have come from. Partly due to their inexperience, and partly because of the malevolent spirit of Jack, their efforts are disjointed and unproductive. Jack and his savages become the dominant force on the island, subverting order wherever they find it. In the end they are even prepared to kill Ralph – a figurehead of order – and only the intervention of the naval officer averts a complete collapse of order.

 EXAMINER'S SECRET
Look at *Lord of the Flies* as a work of art.

FURTHER QUESTIONS

Here are ten more common questions on the novel. Work out what your answer would be to each one, always being sure to draw up a plan first.

❶ Examine the characters of Ralph and Piggy. Explore their relationship as it changes and develops through the novel.

❷ Choose three or four dramatic events. Explain what happens in each and say how you think they might best be portrayed on film.

3 Compare and contrast the characters of Ralph and Jack. How do their characters affect their leadership styles?

4 Imagine that you are Ralph who, having returned home, is telling his adventures to his father. What might he include or leave out? (This could be written in script form.)

5 Choose a character whom you liked or disliked and follow their part in the novel.

6 Examine the part played by the hunters in the story. How important do you think they are? Give reasons to support what you say.

7 The conch and Piggy's glasses are both important items in the story. Look at one of them and the way it contributes to what happens.

8 Look at the character of Simon. Is he an important character or not?

9 Think of the part that death plays in the novel. Why is this subject so central to the story?

10 Examine the ideas of good and evil in *Lord of the Flies*.

DID YOU KNOW?

Golding was fond of pointing out to his students that a barbarian was one who wore a beard – as he did!

Now take a break!

LITERARY TERMS

allegory The depiction of a person close in character and behaviour to someone else who is usually seen in a different context. For example, Jack's dominant and power-hungry manner is often likened to that of Hitler; Simon's eccentricity and kindness are interpreted as Christ-like or akin to a prophet or visionary.

fable A simple story, often using animal characters, with a message or moral which can be seen in, or applied to, everyday life. The primary message, in the context of this novel, is that human beings are naturally capable of evil despite their outward appearance and conditioning towards good/civilised behaviour. (See **original sin** below.)

hypallage Describing something as having a quality or property it cannot possess. For instance, Golding refers to 'the unfriendly side of the mountain' (Ch. 2, p. 43). A mountain is inanimate and so cannot express friendship, although it may appear unwelcoming in some way. This is also known as a transferred epithet.

image, imagery Images are pictures which help to give a greater understanding to the reader. They may be simple similes or metaphors, or more vivid and complex. Simon's cry that he had seen a dead man on a hill provides a direct image of Christ crucified on the hill at Calvary.

irony This can mean saying one thing and meaning something quite the opposite; it may also extend to situations in which one action mocks or ridicules another, when an ill-fated event leads to a more favourable one or vice versa.

metaphor Writers use various devices to help make their meaning clearer to the reader. Simple comparisons, or similes, can be useful; these are usually preceded by 'as' or 'like'. (For example, 'as cold as ice' or 'like a gust of wind'.) Metaphors take the idea of comparison a stage further and describe things as if they had physically changed into something quite different. For instance,

Golding describes the sea as a leviathan, or whale, endowing it with some of the qualities that the creature possesses.

onomatopoeia Some words sound like, and echo, the action they describe, for example 'splash', 'swish' and 'smack'. In *Lord of the Flies* words like 'Zup' and 'Pht' are used to convey the flight of a hurled stone and the sound of a spear.

original sin This is a Biblical reference to Adam and Eve in the garden of Eden, or Paradise, being tempted by the Devil. God would not forgive them and human beings were thereafter recognised as inherently sinful. They must strive and work to be good but being bad is their natural state. Some of the boys on the island revert to this state.

romanticism This is a vague and much abused term which, in the context of *Lord of the Flies*, has nothing to do with the subject of love. It refers rather to those things which are perceived in an unrealistic, emotional or idealised way. For example, both the boys and the naval officer have a 'romantic' notion of what life on the island could be like that is distinctly different from the reality. Ralph's understanding of himself, his innate sense of justice and decency and the supremacy of 'noble' thoughts and ideals in the absence of civilising influences could be viewed as 'romantic'.

subplot The main story-line of any novel is referred to as the plot; any additional story (usually of less significance) is termed the 'subplot'. In *Lord of the Flies* the main plot is what happens to the boys on the island and the two factions which emerge. What happens to Simon; his thoughts, ideas and behaviour as a separate individual, could be regarded as a subplot. Although the main plot and any subplots are different and distinct, it can be seen that they can be interrelated and mutually contribute to the overall action of the novel.

symbolism A symbol is an object or action that can represent ideas and events of wider importance; for instance the conch, glasses or beast.

tri-syllabic chanting During and after hunting the pigs the boys take up a simple and repetitive chant: *'Kill the pig. Cut her throat. Bash her in.'* (Ch. 4, p. 79). Each phrase contains three syllables or beats, the first and third being strongly stressed and the second, or middle syllable, being much weaker. The rhythm produced sounds like a military drum beating 'dum, dee, dum'.

CHECKPOINT HINTS/ANSWERS

CHECKPOINT 1 Conk!

CHECKPOINT 2 He permits him to retain the leadership of the choir.

CHECKPOINT 3 Possibly, since both want such different things: Ralph is concerned about surviving until they can be rescued whilst Jack just wants to enjoy himself.

CHECKPOINT 4 He is probably burned to death.

CHECKPOINT 5 Jack loves hunting!

CHECKPOINT 6 Read carefully the evidence on pp. 51–2.

CHECKPOINT 7 Maurice

CHECKPOINT 8 Ralph is desperate; Jack is jubilant.

CHECKPOINT 9 Their general dirtiness and lack of hygiene

CHECKPOINT 10 In the past Piggy has been bullied and victimised for his asthma and general appearance.

CHECKPOINT 11 His arrival on the island proves that there is life outside and that the war has not annihilated civilisation.

CHECKPOINT 12 The conch is the symbol of civilised authority. It gives freedom of speech which is at the heart of democracy.

CHECKPOINT 13 It enables him to understand the actions of others and to sympathise with them.

CHECKPOINT 14 They are arguing over their courage – or lack of it.

CHECKPOINT 15 He is simply relieved to see the back of him.

CHECKPOINT 16 The voice of authority – one that is always right!

CHECKPOINT 17 He feels concern for the other boys and wants to assure himself that they are safe.

CHECKPOINT 18 They are both washed out to sea.

CHECKPOINT 19 They refer to it as an accident.

CHECKPOINT 20 He avoids discussions and issues orders.

CHECKPOINT 21 The conch

CHECKPOINT 22 Probably, since Jack is keen on hunting pigs and there are close parallels between the deaths of Piggy and those of the pigs.

CHECKPOINT 23 The savagery of the island in general and Jack in particular.

CHECKPOINT 24 His failure to understand the sinister meaning of the stick sharpened at both ends suggest that he cannot imagine they intend to decapitate him and erect his head on a pole.

TEST ANSWERS

TEST YOURSELF (CHAPTERS 1–4)

1 Piggy (*Chapter 1*)

2 Simon (*Chapter 1*)

3 Piggy (*Chapter 2*)

4 Jack (*Chapter 2*)

5 Piggy (*Chapter 4*)

6 Simon (*Chapter 3*)

7 Piggy (*Chapter 4*)

TEST YOURSELF (CHAPTERS 5–8)

1 Ralph (*Chapter 5*)

2 Simon (*Chapter 5*)

3 Maurice (*Chapter 5*)

4 Piggy (*Chapter 5*)

5 Jack (*Chapter 5*)

6 Jack (*Chapter 8*)

7 Simon (*Chapter 8*)

TEST YOURSELF (CHAPTERS 9–12)

1 Piggy (*Chapter 9*)

2 A savage – Jack? (*Chapter 10*)

3 Eric (*Chapter 10*)

4 Ralph (*Chapter 11*)

5 Jack (*Chapter 11*)

6 Sam (*Chapter 12*)

7 Jack (*Chapter 10*)

8 Simon (*Chapter 9*)

9 Ralph (*Chapter 12*)

Maya Angelou
I Know Why the Caged Bird Sings

Jane Austen
Pride and Prejudice

Alan Ayckbourn
Absent Friends

Elizabeth Barrett Browning
Selected Poems

Robert Bolt
A Man for All Seasons

Harold Brighouse
Hobson's Choice

Charlotte Brontë
Jane Eyre

Emily Brontë
Wuthering Heights

Shelagh Delaney
A Taste of Honey

Charles Dickens
David Copperfield
Great Expectations
Hard Times
Oliver Twist

Roddy Doyle
Paddy Clarke Ha Ha Ha

George Eliot
Silas Marner
The Mill on the Floss

Anne Frank
The Diary of a Young Girl

William Golding
Lord of the Flies

Oliver Goldsmith
She Stoops to Conquer

Willis Hall
The Long and the Short and the Tall

Thomas Hardy
Far from the Madding Crowd

The Mayor of Casterbridge
Tess of the d'Urbervilles
The Withered Arm and other Wessex Tales

L.P. Hartley
The Go-Between

Seamus Heaney
Selected Poems

Susan Hill
I'm the King of the Castle

Barry Hines
A Kestrel for a Knave

Louise Lawrence
Children of the Dust

Harper Lee
To Kill a Mockingbird

Laurie Lee
Cider with Rosie

Arthur Miller
The Crucible
A View from the Bridge

Robert O'Brien
Z for Zachariah

Frank O'Connor
My Oedipus Complex and Other Stories

George Orwell
Animal Farm

J.B. Priestley
An Inspector Calls
When We Are Married

Willy Russell
Educating Rita
Our Day Out

J.D. Salinger
The Catcher in the Rye

William Shakespeare
Henry IV Part 1
Henry V
Julius Caesar

Macbeth
The Merchant of Venice
A Midsummer Night's Dream
Much Ado About Nothing
Romeo and Juliet
The Tempest
Twelfth Night

George Bernard Shaw
Pygmalion

Mary Shelley
Frankenstein

R.C. Sherriff
Journey's End

Rukshana Smith
Salt on the snow

John Steinbeck
Of Mice and Men

Robert Louis Stevenson
Dr Jekyll and Mr Hyde

Jonathan Swift
Gulliver's Travels

Robert Swindells
Daz 4 Zoe

Mildred D. Taylor
Roll of Thunder, Hear My Cry

Mark Twain
Huckleberry Finn

James Watson
Talking in Whispers

Edith Wharton
Ethan Frome

William Wordsworth
Selected Poems

A Choice of Poets

Mystery Stories of the Nineteenth Century including The Signalman

Nineteenth Century Short Stories

Poetry of the First World War

Six Women Poets